MORRISING AROUND AMERICA

Joff Summerfield was born in 1967, and grew
in a place called Sutton. The early years of the author's life were ?,
though with time his passions turned and followed the family vein of motor racing. The following years were spent by the author in the all consuming passion
of building a vintage racing Riley special, he managed to accomplish an ambition
by winning race's at some of the country's leading circuits.

Restoring pre war Rolls Royce and Bentleys was the Authors first trade working
in his fathers company for 3 years, until moving out to Toronto in Canada to
work in a drag racing engine company. It was here that the author bought the
hero of his book "Horris" the Morris Minor.

Returning to England, he spent a year working for Mountune racing engines
from where he graduated to building Formula 1 engines for Brian Harts in Har-
low for the following five years. At the end of this time the author became self-
employed within the racing industry specialising in the development and modification of cylinder heads.

By the turn of the millennium though he had become disillusioned with his
work within the racing industry. Just at this time the author had discovered
Greenwich Craft Market, and chose a change of direction in the way he was to
earn his living. Since this time he has made and sold varying crafts at the market.

The author had started cycling again to save money on petrol around town, and
realised that this would be the way to see the countries of the world of which
many of his friends spoke. Being an eccentric traveller the author then built
himself a Penny Farthing bicycle, rode this to Paris for the millennium celebra-
tions, and then rode Lands End to John o'Groats on another Penny Farthing in
September of 2000. The author then embarked on a round the world journey on
his Penny Farthing in 2001. Disaster occurred on the first day when a major
problem occurred with his knees, which stopped the journey. Two years later a
second attempt was made, leaving from Leicester he rode across Europe and
found himself in Budapest when a new knee problem occurred. Never one to
give in, he has now had an operation on the knee and hopes to make another attempt to cycle around the world in the future.

www.pennyfarthingworldtour.com

MORRISING AROUND AMERICA

By

JOFF SUMMERFIELD

Published 2004 by arima publishing

www.arimapublishing.com

ISBN 1-84549-013-4

Printed and bound in the United Kingdom

Typeset in Garamond 12/16

arima publishing
ASK House, Northgate Avenue
Bury St Edmunds, Suffolk IP32 6BB
t: (+44) 01284 700321

www.arimapublishing.com

CHAPTER

ONE

Very cold fingers

The spark for an adventure normally arrives, for me at least, in a burst of thoughts pervading their way across my mind. This is what happened to me one cold and frosty day, whilst lying under a, 1934 Rolls Royce fitting a new, but extremely awkward and heavy exhaust. The train of thought may have been helped along its way by the thump on the head I received when the exhaust slipped, but whatever the cause, my mind had been made up. I knew that the time had arrived to up and leave the family business of vintage car restoration, and head for pastures new, I had received my calling!

So where did I go? Toronto in Canada to be precise, and the first eleven months of my years stay were spent within the city's environs and for the purpose of the story, it is where my unusual adventure did actually begin.

The amazing city of Toronto is an extraordinary place to live, with such a cosmopolitan population numbering over 4.5 million. I enjoyed a wonderful time there. Much to my good fortune, my stay was made exceedingly comfortable, due to the simple and most pleasant reason, that I have family, in the shape of an Aunt and cousin who were willing to endure my presence in their house and lives in this most absorbing period of time for me.

There is an old expression about someone being a fish out of water. Well I can safely say that this fish was not only out of the water, but was lying on the quayside gasping for air at the time I first arrived in Canada. It was I have to say, rather a large culture shock for my poor sensibilities. Upon trying to communicate with the natives for the first time I came across a small, though not hopeless problem. The people seemed to use the same words as me to speak to one another, but somewhere along the line a rather large spanner seemed to get thrown in the works, which tended to make the afore mentioned communication a most entertaining experience. It was rather hard to put a finger on, but I believe the people of North America tended to think and talk from what I can only describe as the balcony of their minds, and then use this method to convey their thoughts to their nearest neighbour. The English mind on the other hand, will tend to lean over its cerebral garden fence so to speak, and gossip to all its neighbours, of course being careful not to be overheard!

Practise makes perfect they say, and with time, the old clockwork motor churning between my ears began to re-tune itself into the Canadian way of thinking. This of course was no bad thing, as it gave me the advantage of being able to use either method of communication, and to evolve my own mid-Atlantic menagerie of expressive thoughts to use for my own pleasure at any given time. Once over this language hurdle, I found that the next quandary to face was to reel myself in from cuffing all the people who asked which part of Australia I was from. Realising that this question was to become a regular part of my daily life, I accepted it, and turned my attention to enjoying some of this wonderful new culture in which I found myself.

Not too long into my stay I came to the administrative decision that although the Toronto public transport system was clean, efficient and on time, it really was, as in all the countries of the world, somewhat of a pain in the posterior to use! The only alternative I had to public transport was of course to beg rides from my family and new friends, who much to my great fortune were always willing to oblige me in this charitable exercise. The only problem with this method is that if you leave it too long, you will then find that the "unspoken ", "pain in the posterior" can catch you up again and land on your own shoulders! So to avoid the possibility of this happening what should a person do? Procure a motor vehicle of course!

The next few weeks were spent searching through all the small ads of the local papers, and what a choice I had before me! Fords, Chevy's, Cadillac's, Olds, Buick's, Pontiac's and these strange ugly looking things called Pacers, but all to no avail. Nothing at all was jumping off of the pages that I searched proclaiming, "buy me", so finally I had to give in, and do what I said one should never do, go straight to the emergency plan B. As far as plans go, I'm sure I won't be remembered for this one in history, simply because plan B consisted of visiting used car lots. So off I set, cash in hand, hope in mind, to buy myself some sort of vehicle. Have you ever had the feeling that you have been walking around all day long with a large sign above your head, with the words "English Fool" flashing away for all to see, because for me it certainly did seem like it.

I found myself entering car lots and fighting my way past all the heaps of rusting Detroit junk, and maybe, and I mean only maybe, spotting something which might at only a most painful pinch do. Then "WHAM " Chuck, (the euphemism I shall use for this type of person), the sharp and slick salesman comes flying over to land on what he thinks is his prey! This is nothing though, because when you open your mouth old Chuck's single (though highly tuned and focused) brain cell goes into overdrive when he realises that he has caught "Limey" man within his net! The sermon that you then receive goes something like this, "Oh Buddy this is such a great car, OK a few holes in the body-work, but that keeps you cool in the summer, yes, you do have to pump the brakes, but hey, all the roads are straight here so you see the corners coming". "What buddy, that large rattling emanating from deep inside the engine, fine adjustment bud, fine adjustment".

In the end I had to let all the many Chucks down, even though they did, without fail splutter to me as I walked off up the road, that theirs was the very best deal in town. In a funny sort of way they were all correct, you see once the "Chuck" grape vine had passed on the news that there was an Englishman on the loose in town looking for a car, each subsequent "Chuck" whom I met came out with progressively more outlandish reasons for me to part with my hard earned currency! Unfortunately for the brotherhood of these people, there are a couple of rules I look to in these situations. One, it doesn't matter how much elbow grease you have got, you still can't polish something you find on your shoe, and two, I have a great affection for the green and crinkly chaps which I exchange for the sweat off my brow at the end of the week. So therefore I really dislike parting with them as we immediately make a special bond together. A no contest situation!

However, when yours smugly was sitting on the bus/train/bus/walk on the way home from the battle of the used car salesmen, it began to dawn on me that I still had no form of transport, only a pocket full of my tightly held money. I then chose to grasp solace from the knowledge that when evenly spread about my lower person, my crinkly comrades in arms did seem to at least make the hard seats of the Toronto public transport system perhaps a little softer!

As the weeks passed by and the despair of having no transport grew larger with each reading of the "For Sales" in the local paper, I resolved to give myself two weeks to find a car. If then at the end of this time, I still had not found a car which I liked, I would take the under $500 section, stick it on the wall, throw a dart, and would acquire whatever, fate or more to the point, my somewhat poor dart throwing would give to me.

Two days before my time was up, I heard the familiar thump on the floor as half an Amazon rain forest, disguised in print as a newspaper, beckoned me to my impending fate with a wall and a dart. While thumbing through the hundreds of pages which made up the gargantuan tome, I couldn't help but wonder why they thought it was necessary to have so many different sections of pure inane waffle to make up this paper, and every day as well. On finding the used car section, I started my usual survey of the columns of yank tanks and started on what by now had become my ritual speed read down the lines, Ford, Ford, Chevy, Caddie, Ford Olds, Ford, Morris Minor, Ford, Pontiac, Chevy, WOOAAAAAAA!!!!!!!! What was that, did my eyes deceive me, was the glutinous mix between my ears playing tricks with me, no, it was true, A Morris Minor! "Alleluia Brothers and Sisters", I heard a strange and unearthly voice shout out, "the man has found his Holy Grail"! My heart was pounding as I read the advert, "1958 Morris Minor, ex district nurse, needs slight attention, fully loaded". OK I thought, do like the song says old son, "Johnny be cool" but it just seemed to be the most perfect car any Englishman could possibly want to ride within while visiting the colonies, but what on earth was "fully loaded"? Visions fluttered through my mind of a car filled up with house bricks, or stuffed full of someone's old junk. The answer to this question lay at the other end of the phone line.

"Fully loaded Buddy, it's got everything, everything". "Are we talking the kitchen sink, junk, diseases, just what are we talking about?" I asked. Once the UN translation system had caught up with the conversation, a large penny or should I say cent, dropped, fully loaded meant that it came with all the factory accessories, but Morris Minors didn't have any, bar a choice of colour! Upon reflection though I surmised it was painted, so strictly speaking it was fully loaded! This line of descriptive shenanigans was duly noted down in the grey cells for future reference and perhaps use!

The following morning I set off with my cousin to see the car. Firstly the street, and then the house were found. I was almost bursting with expectation while waiting to see the car. Then there it was, in its slightly off white paint (ivory in the book), multi coloured wheels, minor dents and rust, and a nice patina of age and non - use. My beaming face turned to look at my cousin, and I have to say I was perhaps a smidgen shocked, "Oh well, shame its such a wreck, but it is cute though" she said. "What!!

Are you blind, can you not see? This car is beyond the point of being splendid, I must have it!"

This loud conversation did not of course particularly help my negotiations with the owner, as he had been standing behind, rubbing his hands as each word passed my lips, so my sudden back tracking into "buying a car mode" left him I feel maybe a tad unconvinced. The realisation soon appeared that he wasn't going to budge from his asking price. Two choices then came to mind, be a total stubborn sod (which by nature I am) not give him any money and go home, or say, "oh well", let him have his asking price, and have that Morris Minor. This was still a surprisingly tough decision for me to take as I really don't like being out suborned, but I of course knew that I had to have that car, so money duly handed over, the car would be delivered on a trailer the following weekend.

The next few days were spent raving to my Canadian friends about my Morris Minor, and this is how Horris the Morris was born. "What the hell's a Horris Minor", I was asked, and so with this mistaken pronunciation, and without a raging priest or even a font being in sight, the Morris was duly christened. The weekend when Horris arrived my friends came round to see what I had bought and I expected them to be duly impressed. Now I had described the car to them as a peoples Rolls Royce, which to me did seem fairly accurate, but upon setting eyes on my new chariot they appeared to give the impression that my powers of description, may have been spoken by someone who had swallowed their rose tinted glasses!

Of course to me it didn't matter in the slightest bit, because I could behold the tremendous potential of my acquisition. I knew the possibilities that lay within the car, and all I then needed to have was the determination to stick to my guns, even in the face of my doubters. This way I knew I could only succeed in the goal, and my goal... well that was obvious, to see Horris the Morris back on the road! Once I had taken the time to have a good look through my new purchase, which is something I probably should have done before parting with my money, I could see that achieving my goal was going to take maybe perhaps a little longer than I had first expected. A few minor problems with the car had come to light, these consisted of such things as a seized engine, the whole wiring system being mostly stripped out, worn out brakes and suspension, rust, cracked wheels and quite a few other less serious things. This did make me realise that it was going to be quite a big job to get finished. At moments of realisation, such that I was experiencing, I was able to thankfully fall back on my old friend, optimism. On this day, thankfully he wasn't merely a small silly piece of optimism, no, he was standing proud, like Caesar in the Coliseum. I also had the knowledge, as I'm sure Caesar did, that no matter what happened, the Christians were going to be eaten by the lions, well Horris was the lion and the other road users the Christians on this day. I felt deeply inside my person, that a Morris had to be the most totally marvellous car to have on the road out in Canada, and I would finish my task no matter what!

Now getting Horris on the highways and byways again did take a lot of time, about three months of effort and stress. Having to pay the equivalent of about £50 for second-hand parts that I knew that I could get from the scrap yard in England for about £5 did hurt me in the pocket region somewhat, not to mention the mental stress of having to shell out all the money. Mechanical things I can handle, if a man made it then a man can fix it, but what nearly sent me over the edge while I worked on Horris, was the weather. My god, did it get cold, you see this was February / March time and Horris was kept in an open carport with no power available. Trying to fiddle with metal parts when its -15 degrees with snow on the ground does tend to test any willpower you may have. I think that the only time that I did go back inside and say "enough is enough" was when trying to undo a seized bolt. I slipped and whacked myself on my frozen lips with my nice large spanner, I still have a small scar, and every now and then I look at it, and remember quite vividly the sight of the spanner heading towards my face with unabated speed. This I took (once warmed up) to be a little test. One cup of coffee later, the bolt was undone, with the same spanner, and I was once again happy with my willpower fully restored. What did make me even happier though was the sight of the bolt flying through the air, having been given its freedom by my caressing hand.

The spanner on the other hand, being a little more expensive, was introduced to his close colleague, Mr Hammer a few and meaningful times, it did learn well from this open and democratic discussion, for neither it nor its friends ever gave any more trouble. As time went on Horris slowly started to come together piece by piece, little by little, and it was rather good to be able to just see a crack of light at the end of the tunnel of my self imposed quest. This was an exceptionally welcome sight for me because the cold was starting to take its toll from my inherent enthusiasm. It wasn't that the eagerness to finish Horris was going it was rather feeling half frozen to the core each night really didn't seem like the most fun thing that I could be doing with my time.

One night while working on Horris, nose running, ears, fingers, and toes, all way past the time when I'm sure frostbite should set in, I sat in the drivers seat and gave myself a good thinking too. I knew of course the best way to get some determination out of myself. It was easy really. Merely imagine all the people that I knew, saying to one another how there was no way I could ever get the car finished. Then the icing on the cake, so to speak, would be the sympathy and the "I did tell you it was a waste of time and your hard earned money". This I would more than likely get when I finally gave up on my mission! It only took about 15 minutes of this reverse positive thinking to give the big roughing up to any doubt I had left in my mind, and from this moment on I knew for certain that Horris the Morris would be finished and eventually hit the North American Highways. If you do have a good streak of determination in you, this reverse positive thinking can be very helpful to use at times. It does, I must admit, annoy you somewhat when you are thinking about it, but afterwards you have so much willpower bursting out of you, there is almost no way that you cannot succeed.

The crack of light became a ray, the ray became a beam, and then with a shower of light we came out of our tunnel, it was MOT time! OK so they're not called MOT's in Canada, you have to have them certified, the cars not the owners that is, (though it had been suggested as an option for me on several occasions), and so Horris was duly booked in for his certification! I knew that Horris needed some welding underneath, so I got the same garage to do the work as who were going to do the certification, this way there was no way they could fail Horris on the welding, because they had done it themselves!

They wanted to have Horris for a few days as they claimed that they were quite busy at the time, and to be honest it was quite nice to have a few days where I couldn't touch the car, or get my hands dirty having to fiddle with something.

Two days later I gave them a call to see if Horris had passed his big test, and yes he had. Goodness, was I a happy fellow, I had achieved my goal, well the first part anyway. The next morning, the second part, the actual driving on the highway was something that I had been really looking forward to with heaps of anticipation. Once I had paid for the welding and the certification I was able to hit the road, Wow! A few miles off down the streets and I suddenly began to realise that the people waving at me weren't classic car fans, but were the type of people who get maybe a little concerned when they see a Morris Minor heading towards them on the wrong side of the road. I was lucky that the garage was situated on a large silent industrial estate and not on a main road. I decided that trying to make them all drive in the left hand lane was perhaps too large a task for me to accomplish in my first drive of Horris, so with a few disgruntled feelings about having to conform, and quite a bit of relief that I hadn't just been flattened by a truck, I pulled over to the right.

Those first few miles back to my Aunt and cousin's house were amazing, and I shall never forget them, rattling along in Horris, with the noise of the engine and the whine of the gearbox and the shaking of the body all reminding me like old friends, why it is I like these old cars. The word for it is character. I felt sorry for the people all in their new identical box shaped cars as we passed them by. They could have no conception of what it is like to drive a real car, certainly one that lets you know through all the various noises and vibrations how it is being treated by its keeper, but that was their loss, and I somehow got the feeling that most of them, but maybe not all, probably wouldn't be able to understand my point of view about the character of a car anyway.

When I had finished this first little run out in the Morris, and had by a certain degree of luck returned home all in one piece, I felt quite amazed that I didn't have any mechanical problems occur on the first drive. I was so happy that I must admit I did chatter on just a bit about this little trip, and the virtues of Morris Minors. By about 10.30 that evening, with my long suffering audience wearing the "blank look" on their faces, I at last took a breath. My audience then strangely disappeared off to bed, and so Horris had to be left for another day.

CHAPTER

TWO

What a splendid idea

The days started to roll by now, it was so good to be mobile again. The Toronto public transport system is clean, efficient and quick, but you still cannot get within a mile, (or kilometre, depending where you are in the world) of the ease you get from owning your own car. Horris really did now have a new lease of life. After sitting around for what I think was quite a few years slowly decaying, he must have thought that his time to visit the great metallic graveyard in the sky was not that far away. I was very pleased to have saved him from a fate worse than rust!

Horris was used throughout the summer mainly for bombing in and around Toronto, and for this he was in his element, ducking and diving in and out of the trams, coaches and yank tanks. It was absolutely splendid fun. The only problem that I found was getting stuck in the tram lines with the skinny tyres that Horris wore, but a quick heave on the huge steering wheel of Horris normally saw us escape with normally only a bump from the vice like grip of the Toronto tram traps! This was also the first time that I came across the phenomena of people pointing and saying, "What the hell is that?" Morris Minors are not a sight that you very often see in North America. This pointing and shouting seemed to happen virtually everywhere that I went, and to be honest I loved it. When stuck in traffic jams with windows open I was forever being asked the afore mentioned question, but what really confused them was when I answered back to their funny looks and pointing fingers. You see, not only had they never expected to see a Morris Minor in North America, but to find one with an Englishman driving, well I think must have been perhaps a little unbelievable for some of them considering the astonished looks I received from more than a few of my fellow road users. I think quite a lot of ex-pats and British holiday makers must have thought that I had taken a seriously wrong turn somewhere in England to end up here,

or even been sucked up by some strange Wizard of Oz type phenome-
non, and deposited in North America. It has rained frogs and fish before
now you know, but a shower of Minors would perhaps be stretching it a
little.

Towards the end of the year that I was spending in Canada I started to
think about what I was going to do with Horris when finally leaving, and
after much deliberation I came up with two possible choices. The first
was to have him shipped home, which would be great, as I doubt that
there are to many left hand drive Morris Minors in England. The cost was
a bit of a setback though at around $2000, and Horris would have to be
shipped from New York. The second option, then started to gestate in
the inner sanctums of my cranium, was maybe to go for a drive! Ok,
when I say drive what I mean is to go for a really serious drive, the sort
that I would never forget. In my time in Canada I had never ventured
south into the USA, not for any particular reason you understand, I
merely hadn't bothered. This though would be the perfect opportunity to
go and have a nice motoring tour around America! The latter idea seemed
to be, after somewhat little deliberation, the best thing that I could possibly do and I announced to roars of laughter, that this was to be my plan.
Having proven at the start of the year that it was possible to get the car
going again I was quite shocked at this reaction. The questioning of my
sanity had been a long term recurring theme, but obviously I hadn't quite
shown that I had completely regained it again after the exposure to the
cold weather at the start of my stay.

Now started a morale boosting game of sweepstakes as to how far I
would actually get. The first bets came in, the Toronto city limits ("huh"),
then Niagara Falls, (several times, a popular bet that one). A person with
obviously great confidence in me then chose Buffalo, which was at least
actually inside the States. The final bets came in and I think that my family, and I hope that it wasn't only due to loyalty, put their money down
with an extravagant gesture to all the other unbelievers, on the, some
might perhaps say radical long shot of New York! This I have to mention
was appreciated by yours truly, as they did then open themselves up to a
certain degree of ridicule from the so-called better informed members of
this particular group of gamblers. I myself wanted also to bet, but it
caused a degree of consternation along the lines of possible match fixing,
when I explained exactly on where I was to place my bet. It was unilater-
ally allowed with the accompaniment of again a certain amount of hilarity.

My money was placed on California!

Having stated to all and sundry my great confidence in making it the whole way to the Sunshine State, I thought it best that I actually did a few sensible preparations to Horris to make sure that there was a chance that my boast would become reality.

Being on a very tight budget, I chose that the best way to save money would be to spend a lot of the trip sleeping in Horris. Now Morris minor saloons aren't all that universally renowned for their spacious interiors, so some modifications would have to be made to my new sleeping compartment. I then set about a series of trials to find a way of comfortably sleeping in the car, and they went something like this. I firstly tried lying out across the back seats, but this forced me to lie with my knees around my ears, and if I wanted to turn over in the night, which I always do, I would have to sit up and point my head in the other direction. The next plan was to try lying across the front seats, again this led to failure as the gear stick, handbrake, and gap between the seats left me once again no room to stretch out. This was proving to be a major problem. A period of time passed with a certain amount of head scratching going on, but thankfully I managed to come up with a reasonable answer to this teasing conundrum. The passenger seat was fixed to the floor by four bolts, these I removed and replaced with studs and wingnuts, thus enabling me to quickly remove the passenger seat from inside the car without a great deal of fuss. The now liberated seat could be then placed where the driver normally sits, leaving a nice open area from the footwell to the front of the rear seat squab. The clever bit of this particular master plan now came into force, pulling out the back seat squab; it could then be turned lengthways and fitted into the space left vacant by the missing passenger seat. It was an absolutely perfect fit. All that was then needed was to have a small cushion to level things up in the dip in the floorpan where the squab used to be. Then with a fair amount of ease I found that I could almost stretch out fully lying lengthways in the car! On recounting the plan to various outdoor Canadian types, it was suggested to me that It probably would be a good idea if I were to try out my sleeping arrangements for at least one night before setting off, but as I explained to them, I really couldn't find any other option which would allow me to sleep in the car with even a tiny degree of comfort, so whether this worked or not it would have to do.

The only other interior modification that I made to the car was to fit a carpet, but again due to my budget constraints I had to do the trimming myself, as buying a new carpet from England, or having someone here make one was a goodly mile outside of my budget. The call was put out on the grapevine for anyone that had an old piece of antique Persian rug that I could cut up to fit into the car. Unfortunately none materialised, so I had to make do with a large piece of white deep pile carpet that had been in someone's garage for a while. The carpet proved to be most excellent for the task, though it did show itself to be a blister inducing swine to cut and shape to the floorpan of the car.

I now moved on to the exterior of the vehicle. Of course I came up with a very sound theory for this part of my strategy, which was, if I made it look all shiny and polished, all the thieves, robbers and bandits of the road and of the mountains, would see Horris and I as their pots of gold. This I thought was rather solid judgement, but merely to make sure I put an external padlock on the drivers door and a drawbolt on the inside of the passenger door. The extra security would enable me to lock myself in (having wound down the window and reached out for the padlock) and also when leaving the car I wouldn't have to rely solely on the original Morris locks.

The final touch to the new super secure Morris was to fit a hidden ignition switch as well as the normal one. Using all my cunning, I placed it behind the speedometer, so when leaving the car on its own you would pull out the speedo from the dash, click off the switch and replace the instrument back into the dashboard. Thus Horris was protected from any international Morris Minor thieves that might be lurking about! The final preparations were fairly simple really; merely a case of changing things that I thought may give me trouble while on the road. The clutch was the first to be replaced of these items, and to my horror, while under the car doing the job; I noticed the welding that the garage had done to the chassis for me at the start of the year. It was absolutely abysmal! They had only tacked on a piece of tin over the old rotten front chassis leg and I could move the bottom part of the suspension where it went into the supposed solid part of the chassis. Time was running out and I was due to leave in a couple of days, so I used my power of being a silly fool, and determined that as the suspension hadn't managed to fall off in the past year it would probably last another 30 or so days! The engine mounts and a new timing chain were the last mechanical things that I had to do before I set off. These duly replaced, we were virtually on the starting grid.

The last couple of days ticked by before my departure date, and these managed to include a mad dash about the countryside trying to secure some car insurance. The previous company that I had been using, who had charged me an extortionate fee, had decided that they wouldn't insure me for one more month, especially if I intended to go to the States. Loads of calls and a fair degree of panic later I did manage to find someone to cover me, though I couldn't find anyone to give me insurance for only 30 days. The shortest period that anybody would offer me was six months. The way I managed to get around this was by paying in monthly instalments by direct debit from the bank. Strangely enough I had a feeling that my account would be empty come the due date of the second instalment!

CHAPTER

THREE

The journey begins

The day was the 25th of November; one that I had been counting down to with a great deal of trepidation, but now it was here. The past year that I had spent in Toronto had been fantastic. Living with my Aunt and cousin and meeting all these wonderful new people had made it an incredibly wonderful experience for me, and one that I shall never forget.

Well the time came when I had to leave, and I have to say It wasn't all that much fun, especially as I was heading out into the unknown, having no real idea of what lay ahead. I never have liked saying goodbye to people in this type of situation; it always seems so final. The last week had been full of this stress and I was glad that my family were the last goodbyes that I had to endure. It is rather strange really; I'm your typical Englishman when it comes to emotions, you know, "for gods sake don't show any"! The stupid stiff upper lip and all that nonsense can be somewhat of a chalice around the neck. Having spent the last year in a multi cultural society which has a great deal of Latin blood flowing through its veins I was fairly pleased that this had seemed to have rubbed off on me to a certain degree. Yes I did shed a tear as I drove off. I think that Canada and its people have helped me down the path to showing some emotions, though I do readily agree that I still have a fair way to go along that particular avenue.

When I packed the car in the morning I only just about managed to squeeze everything in, this of course typically being the first time I had tried loading the car with all the encumbrances that I had managed to accumulate over the previous year. The only problems that I could now foresee were my sleeping arrangements, these of course having been calculated with an empty car. Now that it was full to the brim with all of my junk, I felt that I might have problems in the sleeping department that night!

As it was the 25th of November, it of course was somewhat cold and slippery, and so with care I drove out of Don Mills (which was the suburb of Toronto that I had been living in) for the last time. Passing familiar places flooded me with happy memories of the previous year; I knew the journey had started. I turned onto the Highway 401 and headed downtown.

My first official stop of the trip was at the CN Tower, this being the worlds tallest free standing building. The view from the "space deck" at the very top is quite breathtaking, looking out over Lake Ontario on one side, and from the other, the view of the gleaming city of Toronto. Looking directly down you also get an amazing view into the baseball stadium, the little specks playing this perplexing game with the rules that I still actually don't understand, is quite surreal. Quite the best time to visit the building is at nightfall, as the lights from the city and from the boats on the lake are quite remarkable. I parked Horris as close as I could to the tower to take my first photos. The only problem I suddenly found was that because of the great height of the tower, I really couldn't get Horris in the picture as well. I drove around to the other side of the Baseball stadium, and this gave me a better perspective for the shot. I only hope it was worth all the trouble.

Horris looking up to the CN Tower

When I had taken the first photo it almost felt like I had ticked off the initial task from my "non existent" roster. Saying goodbye to Toronto I pulled onto the Queen Elizabeth Highway and pointed Horris towards Niagara Falls. Off we set at our leisurely pace following the edge of Lake Ontario. Passing the outskirts of Mississauga, named after the previous indigenous inhabitants, I remembered that it was a place a lot of, though not all, Torontarians seem to turn their noses up at. Having visited friends who lived in this area, it did seem to be only another slightly run down suburb that is adjacent to a big city. The pattern I think is repeated the world over, and is always found to be of good use as a piece of self indulgent snobbery for the people who live in the better areas. I drove onwards through Oakville and Burlington, places that I had never stopped to visit before or now, as they were unfortunately towns that were on the way to somewhere and never a destination. We crossed the impressive bridge that cuts off the very tip of Lake Ontario and passed through Hamilton. Horris was just purring along at that moment and I could feel the butterflies in my stomach as Niagara Falls and the border drew ever closer.

Having come across a sign on the QEW highway pointing off to Balls Falls, it reminded me that it was a location that friends and I had visited in the summer. The falls are set in some lovely parkland with the river running along one side. A short trudge by the side of the overgrown and wooded riverbank and you arrive at the spectacular falls themselves. They are about 30 feet high and about 50 feet across, and were inhabited on the day that we visited by a group of what seemed like suicidal young men determined to kill themselves by leaping from the top! The spectacle obviously was great entertainment for us, and it didn't detract from the beauty of the surroundings. It was actually more of a contrast. The balance between the danger and the splendour before us made the whole situation quite intriguing, and what's more in a country of total commercialism, it was gratifyingly free! The next stop on that day was the town of Thorold, which was your typical small backwater community with the cars all parked nose to pavement along the high street, yet I noted at the time the severe lack of people on the streets, so who owned the cars I really couldn't fathom. We then strolled into a small diner to attempt to replenish our empty stomachs, this was a bit of a hit and miss operation as you could only tell it was open by the fact that the lights were switched on. Upon reaching the inner sanctums, the few patrons of this obviously fine establishment gave us some rather strange but not hostile looks. There was a bar, a few tables with menus and ashtrays, and of course the very thing that we were expecting, a single lane ten pin bowling alley! The alley was squeezed down one wall and out into an extension that they must have built to house this piece of local enterprise. I could only imagine the scene in this bar on a Saturday night, booze, smoke, huge hamburgers, and good old boy, thigh slapping country hospitality. We ordered the obligatory hamburgers with all the extras, and they arrived fifteen minutes later. At this point in time my vision of a hamburger was something that McDonalds produced. What arrived seemed so huge by comparison I was quite staggered. Had they just shaved the cow, roasted him and then put him in a bun for me to eat. The image of the chef going through this process did, I admit, bring a rather silly smirk to my face. The thing that I find strange with North America in general is that there are so many commendable small restaurants that people can use and get a huge meal that tastes good for a small price. Yet, because of the convenience of the fast food chains, they prefer to use those, very strange indeed.

As I drove into Niagara town the 2100 ft wide Horseshoe Falls came into sight. Flowing around 195,000 cubic feet of water a second, they make for a stunning sight. The town though did seem somewhat unusual, all the times I had been there before it had been the height of the tourist season, and the place had been packed. Now at the end of November at around ten in the morning there was nobody about, it reminded me of my home town of Southend in the off season, all we needed were a few tumble weeds to finish the picture. I pulled up alongside the falls and got out to have a closer inspection. Although I had seen them before, today's view was in a completely new context, it was the first day of my adventure and they were my first major natural sight. Standing at the very edge where the water from Lake Ontario crashes downwards into the start of Lake Erie, the natural forces that you are witnessing are quite overpowering, almost trying to suck you over for having the audacity to come so close. As the clear mass of water plummets over the edge and downwards, you can only imagine the bravery or maybe the foolhardiness of the people who have made it their mission in life to ride the falls in a barrel. Had I been one of those people standing there on a cold November morning, knowing that the next time I was to be near that edge I would be going over it in a potential round shaped coffin, I think that convincing myself it was a silly idea would have been quite easy to accomplish, losing face would be a lot more palatable than losing life!

It was now time to take the second set of photos of Horris in the foreground of a famous sight. As I said before the whole place was virtually deserted so lining my four-wheeled friend up for the pictures was quite simple. Not only was I able to do loads of rushing to and fro, and a great deal of repositioning to get the shot that I wanted, but joy of joys, there were no large (in size and in numbers) pink families of tourists all standing around in the way of my obviously rather important photographic shoot!

In awe of the falls

I then proceeded to pack up my equipment, well, OK I put my camera back in my pocket, and then pointed Horris towards our next destination, America!

Horris and I motored across the Peace Bridge that spans the river about half a mile downstream from the falls. Half way across there are two flags, one being the Maple leaf and the other the stars and stripes. Crossing now into the States and leaving Canada, I felt a sharp twinge of emotion coursing its way through my body. The feeling that now I was leaving behind the past year of joy, friendship and wonderful experiences, and whatever laid ahead of that second flag filled me with trepidation and excitement. If the truth be known what did lay beyond the second flag was the American border customs control. Here I had a slight sense of foreboding, as although I did have a visa, I had also outstayed my 90 days that you can officially stay in Canada by a mere 244 days, so I was rather hoping that the Americans wouldn't hold this against me. I guessed that if

I drove in with a grin on my face, and looked moderately un-threatening perhaps they might actually allow me to enter. I pulled up to the border post, which reminded me of the toll booths at the Dartford tunnel, and handed over my passport. The extremely serious and stern looking State Trooper had a long look and told me to go over and park by the large building and report inside. I did wonder for a moment whether or not to make a run for it, as I am sure they had decided that I looked much too dishevelled to be allowed in, and probably the thumbscrews would be awaiting me inside the building. The thought of being chased by probably 20 or 30 police cars with sirens blaring did in a strange way appeal, as I'm sure that Horris and I could easily out run them. Also when they started shooting, I did actually know that they always miss the person that they are chasing, I have seen it happen on many occasions on the television! Although the big chase scene was quite enticing, I chose to play them at their own game, call their bluff and enter the building. I bet my last Canadian dollars with myself that this would completely wrong foot them. They wouldn't know what to do, and in their confusion they would allow me to enter the USA without asking too many questions. I walked through the door and across a large chequered tile floor (easy to clean after interrogations) to a wide counter that had placed on it, exactly as I had expected, a spotlight! OK it wasn't switched on, but I knew that at any moment the powerful bulb could be burning into my eyes!

"Hi, how can I help you?" Trick question no doubt, so I said in my most casual James Bond type voice, "Can I come into your country please", and handed the ~~pleasant and cheerful~~, mean and dangerous looking man behind the counter my passport. He looked hard at the page that contained the visa, then looked up at me and said, (this was obviously to be the start of the interrogation) "how long will you be staying in the USA?" I answered immediately before he had even had chance to catch his breath, with a cutting "Only one month officer." He retorted in the way only a highly trained international interrogator can reply to an answer like that. "I'm not an officer, I'm a customs official, and welcome to America". I can only guess that I had been lucky enough to cross the border on the day when one of our British spy customs officials was on duty, so I gave him the special English wink to let him know that I completely understood, and left the building with a bullish smile upon my face. I find it very amusing to see unwary people have problems at customs, and I do believe that this is normally due in no small part to their own paranoia, unlike me of course!

These histrionics had taken a mind draining half an hour, but now I was in America, they had actually let me in, amazing! This to me was the first major hurdle passed as I had expected to be told that the combination of a Limey and a Morris Minor, even a nice one called Horris, would be too much for Uncle Sam to bare, and I would be turned round and sent on my way back to Toronto with a flea in my ear. Now as the quaint old saying goes this is where the bullshit stops, I'm in, and on my way!

I now drove into the town of Buffalo, which is the first dwelling on the other side of the border crossing and one of the leading flour milling cities in the USA. I then resolved to stop at my first American garage to fill up with petrol. Having stood there for five minutes clicking the pump without the slightest drop of fuel coming out, I noticed that the man in the garage window waving at me. Obviously the pump that I was trying to use was out of order, so I replaced it and moved on to the next one and tried again. The same thing proceeded to happen once more, so I entered the building of the waving attendant to investigate. It became clear when I went inside, in the USA, unlike Canada or England, you have to pay for your petrol before you actually put it in the car, and then if necessary go and collect your change. This can of course mean queuing twice, which seemed rather peculiar for this fast food etc. nation.

With a full tank I headed out of town on the Interstate 90 in the rough direction of the East coast. My route planning consisted of the following, in the morning I would look at the map and decide where I probably was, then scrutinise the area to see any famous places that I might have heard of within a days drive and head in that direction. This solved any problems of getting lost from my route as I didn't really have one in the first place to get lost from, so no doubt this system would allow me to trundle along in a permanent and happily bewildered state! Heading away from Buffalo I was running parallel with the south shore of Lake Ontario and through New York State. The road was very straight and yes amazingly most of the traffic here does tend to stick to 55 - 60 mph which was great for me as this was just about my cruising speed.

I passed the town of Rochester. The land on which it is built was bought from the Seneca people in 1779, and then resold in 1803 to one Nathaniel Rochester who then modestly named the new settlement after surprisingly, himself. There were signs for the originally named Veedersburg but now called Amsterdam and Rotterdam, these names sounded familiar but I couldn't quite remember from where. About 10 miles outside of the city of Syracuse my stomach alarm rang with the intelligence that it was about time it was filled with a large amount of food, so I pulled into an enormous drive in diner come truck stop. In the car park I met what appeared to be a French Canadian and his son, though unless they were also using my method of navigation, they were more likely to be Americans. Of course they could have been in the woods for a long time and were simply rather lost, which would possibly explain the front of their old Jeep, for strapped to it were two huge (small horse size) deer. "Bin hunting," he grunted to me as I looked at the poor creatures. How he could claim shooting them with a large rifle fitted with telescopic sights from probably a 100 yards as "hunting" I really couldn't under-stand. It really seemed like a form of macho American bullshit. As I walked away I only hoped it wasn't Rudolf and Dasher strapped to the front of his Jeep, as poor old Santa would have to miss a few houses out this year while doing his rounds. If that was the case, I could think of a father and son who would deserve to miss out on their presents at Christmas. I didn't actually say this to their faces, for fear of joining my friends on the front of the Jeep, and besides, being murdered on the first day of my trip because of a tactless comment, would instantly loose me my bet with my chums back in Toronto.

After a big sickly fry up, I once more hit the I-90 heading now for Al-bany as my days final destination. A few miles after the town of Utica, the road took up position alongside the 150 mile long Mohawk River that flows along until finally emptying into the Hudson. I followed the Mo-hawk all the way until we were north of the town of Schenectady. Most of the people that I had spoken to before I set off had told me that this part of the trip would be rather boring scenery wise. I have to contradict them though, because I found this part of the country, although not to be abso-lutely stunning, it represented a very pleasant rural scene for most of my ride along the I-90. On leaving my guide, the Mohawk River, who had a previous engagement to turn north, I motored on for a few more minutes until I was only a small number of miles outside Albany. I had deter-mined to stay out of the downtown areas when sleeping in Horris, mainly due to the "being murdered" factor which had been beaten into me by everyone before I had departed. A quick twitch of the wheel had us pulled off the road and into a service station having according to Horris's speedo, covered 360 miles in the first day. The speedo did tend to wave about a bit between 40 and 70 mph while you drove along, so a little bit of guesstimation had to be used to judge your speed, though this wouldn't effect the mileage readings. I must confess that it didn't used to do this, it is only since deciding in a bored moment to overhaul the speedo that it started to happen, but it would give me something to fix if the need or urge ever arrived.

CHAPTER

FOUR

The Muzzle of a gun

I had now spent my first night sleeping in Horris. Well, it was what you might say a rather interesting and active few hours. My first, and an important lesson which I learnt last night was, don't ever try and sleep across the front seats. I was rather tired when I arrived in my parking spot for the night and couldn't be bothered to move all the seats about into their pre-arranged sleeping positions. Foolish mistake! Slumbering on the front seats really doesn't work, it's uncomfortable, you can't sleep, and it's just a downright pain in the nether regions (depending on the exact location of the gearstick!), so from now on I would definitely use my predetermined and carefully thought out sleeping system. The second lesson of the night was that when you are half frightened to death, have a handy paper bag at the ready to breath deeply into to help prevent hyperventilation! Let me explain. By about two in the morning my exhaustion had overcome the uncomfortable deficiencies of Horris's two front seats and I was getting batches of about 20 minutes of snoozing between having to move. It was between one of these sound asleep moments that I became aware of a car pulling up beside me in the carpark. Being rather brave, I managed to close my eyes even tighter and pull my head further into the sleeping bag using the well known "brave man" technique of "ignore it and it will go away". Unfortunately this did not deter my now super sensitive hearing, and I heard voices and a car door open. The ground in the carpark was gravel and I heard every single one of the crunching footsteps as they strode around Horris until they arrived back at the drivers door by my head. More mumbled voices then cerbang, clank, rattle went the door handle as someone tried to get in "Oh dear", was the first thought that crossed my mind as I was trying to remember where I had put the ignition keys ready for a hasty escape. I fumbled an arm out of the sleeping bag and located the keys on the floor, then disaster! I remembered that I had switched off my secret ignition switch that was hidden behind the speedo when I had gone to get some food, so before I could make a daring getaway this would have to be switched back on! As this takes about a minute to do I realised that the murderers outside the car would have more than enough time to do as their titles suggested! As these panic-stricken thoughts were bouncing around inside my mind I heard a metallic clunk clunk on the window above my head, I knew now that it was time to face my executioner, so with the type of heroics that you would probably only normally see on a battlefield, I did a very manly thing,,,,,, I opened my eyes!

"ARRGGGGGG" I shouted as the torch shone into my ocular regions and the muzzle of the gun that had been doing the clunking on the window came into view. At this point my heart seemed quite intent on extracting itself from my chest and probably also the East coast of America, going by the rate that it was pounding within me. Then only moments before I was about to get dressed, put my shoes and socks on, leap out of the car, and wrestle my gun wielding psychopathic assailants to the ground (having probably already taken the first six bullets from the gun), I heard him say in a blood curdling American drawl, "Police officer, open the door"! It has to be said, that this did come as a rather small relief to my person, though the warrior inside me was of course quite disappointed it had missed out on going into battle (I think!). Sheepishly winding down the window I was met by a rather pleasant officer. His envisioned co-murderers that he had been speaking to were nothing more than a radio in his squad car. The funny thing that he then said to me was that he was merely checking to see if I was dead or not. Well, little did he know that he had very nearly killed me himself from good old-fashioned fright. He mentioned in a somewhat kindly drawl that he would stop by again later on in the morning to see if I was OK, and my request perhaps to give me a quick blare on the siren when he did come back so I knew it was him, was accepted but with a degree of puzzlement.

I rose early that morning and partook of a good truckers breakfast in the local diner. I gave Horris what was to be his first of many regular morning checks of oil, water etc. and then once more set upon the Interstate 90. I passed Albany, the previous home to the Mohican Indian tribe before the European invasion, without stopping and crossed the Hudson River so named after Henry Hudson who explored it in1609.

I drove onwards passing over the state line to the West of Pittsfield, a sign by the roadway informing me that the town had a population of

50,174, and was named after William Pitt, 1st Earl of Chatham.

A few minutes after eight o'clock, Horris and I crossed over into Massachusetts, which was the sixth state to join the union in 1788. Unfortunately our arrival was over 200 years too late for the party, but at least we had actually made it to the second state on the itinerary. I agreeably pondered that the odds on just how far I could manage to travel would now be shortening back in Toronto.

When I had passed through the city of Springfield so named in 1640, the weather chose to give me a little trouble. Firstly it started with a small falling of drizzle, which of course was not a problem for Horris as he was designed to live in a drizzly climate, but then it changed in an instant and I found myself within the grasps of a good old-fashioned North American thunderstorm. After only probably half an hour of driving through the storm the wipers decided to cry enough. This occurrence I found rather frustrating, as it was a problem I had foreseen before my departure, so had taken the precaution of fitting a replacement wiper motor. I steered Horris from the roadway onto the hard shoulder and peered with a look of displeasure under his bonnet to see if there was anything that could be quickly fixed. I took a moment to have a good fiddle around with various items, but ended up having to use an extremely technical procedure to repair the somewhat delicate workings of the Morris wiper system. I pulled one off!

Thus friction duly cut in half, the newly divorced wiper once more got back to its proper job of water removal. I now of course had succeeded in reducing my vision through the screen by half, but soon discovered the correct manner in which to gain a non-blurred view of anything on my right hand side (Horris being left hand drive). All that was necessary I found, was for me to push my nose and left side of my face against the screen and peer across the bonnet, thus restoring the full horizon of my scenic intake! Having therefore repaired the wipers, I was well-nigh about to pull away from the hard shoulder when a police car came into view in the mirror and started to flash his lights and blow his siren at me in a most belligerent manner. I immediately swung open the car door and jumped out onto the side of the roadway, this is a technique I have had cause to use with great effect on many an occasion. Throwing the policeman off guard, it generally helps to prevent getting a fine for not wearing a seatbelt. I had been previously warned though by friends back in Toronto, that using this procedure and rushing up to the police car may end up with me getting a gun muzzle pointed in my direction from the wary Sheriff. So with this in mind, I made a slow and most innocent look-

ing stroll to his door so as to enquire about which one of the deadly sins
it was that I had committed. As it turned out the rather amicable policeman had only stopped to see if I had a problem. When I said that sitting
on a Morris Minor seat for three hours had been giving me a bit of an
aching arse problem, my sarcasm was absorbed with rather a dour blank
look. Having now confused him I then enlightened him with my real predicament, which he happily accepted and sent me on my journey with not
so much as a single flea in either of my ears. As I pulled away, I consid-
ered how the blank look on his face had seemed all too familiar to the
ones I had received in Canada every time that I had communicated with a
new native. It reminded me that the North American populace when en-
countering an Englishman and attempting to converse, seem to have a
real problem with understanding him and his humour. The vocal difficulties do leave you repeating yourself for much of the time, though on this
occasion even though he was quite friendly, I thought it best not to try.

The last part of the I-90 between Springfield and Boston is actually,
ignoring what I had been told before I left, a very nice and scenic ride
running through the Adrondike mountains all the way to my next destination of Boston.

As I motored into the city, I did find quite a contrast with its character
after becoming used to the ever so modern Toronto. The buildings were
a mix of 1940's skyscrapers and single story town houses, giving an air of
fairly relaxed bustle. It was here that I nearly managed to have my first
accident. Driving across one particular road intersection, cars seemed to
be coming at me from all directions accompanied by shouts and blowing
of horns. When it happened I did think it to be a rather strange and
somewhat dangerous way to go about your business, until I noticed that
there were traffic lights strung by wires high up across the road. Having
now spotted these, and chosen to obey the different colours, especially
the red ones, my progress along the roads of Boston did become safer,
though a great deal less exciting! My next task, now that I had actually
made it into the city was to find the youth hostel. Unfortunately I only
had a large-scale map of America and a very bad YHA street plan. This
proved to be a pain as neither of them showed that half of the streets are
one way, which was all rather confusing for someone who was born
without any proper sense of direction. After about an hour of what
seemed like endless searching, I eventually did come across the hostel.
Well, to be totally truthful, I pulled over to the side of the road, as I knew
that it must have been pretty close, and had one last inspection of the
map. As luck would have it on this occasion, it turned out I had stopped

right outside the hostel's front door!

The sign on the aforementioned door informed me that the hostel wasn't going to be open until 1 o'clock, so with an hour to kill before being allowed to enter, I parked up in a side street, went and procured a rather healthy donut for my lunch, and came back to sit in Horris and have a bit of a snooze.

I didn't pay much attention when a truck pulled up in front of me to park, or so I thought. He was in actual fact a tow truck, and was only about to try and tow me away as I had inadvertently stopped in a no parking area. The fellow was amazingly fast; he had the hooks around Horris's front suspension before I even had a chance to wind down the window to exclaim my disapproval. Even when I managed this it seemed to make very little difference, he was on a real mission. The only option left to me was to start Horris up and engage in a tug of war with the truck, this thankfully did get his attention and after an abundance of cursing and shouting in my direction he released Horris and carried off the car that was parked behind. So it was with a climax of vexation that I discovered that the hostel had no parking of any sort, and with my encounter with the tow truck still fresh in my mind I wasn't about to leave Horris parked upon the street. Knowing now to perhaps phone ahead in future, I resolved that my safest option was to sleep somewhere outside of town, so with camera and car in hand I set of on a whistle stop tour of Boston. My first port of call was the Cheers bar made famous by the television show of the same name. Here of course I had to have a picture of Horris in front of the building. I parked up across the road and waited until a taxi pulled away and left a gap. Seizing the opportunity of an opening space, I shot across the oncoming traffic and made it into a prime position parked before the front door. Having vaulted out of Horris's door I was immediately accosted by a bumptious fellow telling me that I must not under any circumstances park where I had left Horris! I then quickly rambled to him that as the Morris was a classic car it was exempt from any such parking restrictions under Boston city law. By the time that I had dashed back across the road with camera and picture in hand, he was still flustering about how he had never heard of this particular law, and how he would definitely find out if it was true or not. So I apologise in advance to any classic car owners who pull up to the foreground of the Cheers bar in the future and experience a disagreeable doorman!

The Cheers bar

The next place of interest on the city tour was to go and see the vessel where the Boston tea party had taken place. On the way, while stationary at some traffic lights which I had fortunately noticed, a young Indian cab driver wound down his window and told me about his father who owned a Morris back in Delhi. He was extremely surprised to see a Morris in Boston, and told me that it made him feel rather homesick for his family and country. My new friend pointed me in the right direction for the harbour front and off I set, metaphorically carrying my cup in hand, hoping that the Tea party hadn't finished without me.

The tea party took place on not one, but three ships, on December 16th 1773, when the local colonists dumped our lovely English tea into the harbour as a protest against a tax that had been imposed upon them by our parliament. This act of Tea destruction and the Boston massacre of three years earlier, all helped lead to the start of the American Revolution, or revolt as it was then known upon British shores.

The rest of the afternoon was spent motoring around the city occupied in taking photos of interesting buildings, and eating uninteresting food. The day drawing to a close, I looked to the earlier knowledge that my best option for a place to enjoy my slumbers would be somewhere out of town, so I found my way to the interstate 93 which took me almost immediately past the town of Quincy a few minutes to the south of Boston. Heading now west for about ten further miles I turned once more in a Southerly direction onto the I-95 heading for Providence town. Once I started to enter into the town's limits, the search started for a garage to acquire some petrol as Horris was starting to get a little bit low on fuel. I now once again found myself lost, driving around in an attempt to find somewhere that was open and willing to sell me some of the required liquid. Forty five minutes later my senses were rather pleased that Providence is a very nice and pretty town, as I had just driven around a good deal of it in my little search for the sustenance required by my machine, but happily I was now back on the I-95 heading South with a full tank and a spring in my step (or my tyres!).

My road passed into the state of Connecticut and as it was getting quite late, and the eyes in my head were starting to droop, it seemed like a good idea to pull off the roadway and find somewhere to lay my head. The next road I came across heading off the I-95 was to a place called Groton. Here I found a large truckers Burger bar and parked up. Once I had greedily partaken in the heart attack inducing food on offer, I set to on Horris to get the sleeping arrangements organised in the way that I had previously planned before setting out on the journey. This accomplished I was remarkably pleased knowing that I would at least have a comfortable nights sleep. Regrettably though, the temperature did seem to be getting lower each day even though we were heading South, which did start to cause me some concern, as freezing to death wasn't too high on my "things to accomplish" list! The second day of the drive was now over and we had clocked up a respectable 282 miles.

CHAPTER

FIVE

Those Yellow Devils

The new day dawned bright and early, at about half past six to be precise. The sun was shining but a sharp chill hung in the air. I knew that I had a rather exciting day ahead of me, and I must admit, I also felt a little bit of apprehension because this was the day that Horris the Morris and yours truly took on New York city!

While I was still parked up in Grotons fine Burger eating establishment I thought it fairly prudent to go through Horris with a moderately fine tooth comb, I checked all the fluid levels, as I had done every morning so far, and also reset the distributor points, all this to carefully tune the car ready for his forth-coming battle against the demon Yellow cabs! Off we set down the Interstate 95 once more, and straight away felt quite at home, why was this you ask? I had just crossed the river Thames into New London! The city was originally settled and named by the unimaginative John Winthrop in 1646, and even has its very own boat race held every year between Yale and Harvard universities. Meeting with this piece of nostalgia caused a goodly ripple of merriment across my face and inner person. My joy was then abated when someone, somewhere, determined that it was time to get serious with us! Much to my immediate displeasure, Horris's engine started getting somewhat hot and also seemed to be losing power. Could this be the first breakdown predicted by all my friends back in Toronto? I sincerely hoped not. Pulling off the road, the bonnet was immediately raised up to investigate the problem. My first suspect was the ignition system being out of adjustment because of the high engine temperature, but no, after checking both the timing and the distributor I had to look elsewhere as these were both fine. After a goodly amount of head scratching, my prognosis was that the needle valve in the carburettor float chamber was sticking, thus causing the engine to run lean, i.e. hot, which equals less power, and was also the reason Horris had spat back out of the carburettor a number of times. So using the highly advanced tool "The encouragement stick" or "hammer" by its more common name, I "encouraged" the float chamber a couple of times to free the needle off. Then having started the motor with some trepidation Horris instantly fired up and happily ran perfectly for the rest of the day!

A few miles after New London the I-95 starts to run parallel with the Atlantic coastline. Here you can smell the clean sea air as it billows in from the ocean. Strangely enough, the taste of the air actually made me feel somewhat homesick, as I knew that the only thing between home and myself was now the ocean. Even with Horris being such a splendid car as he undoubtedly was, he still would be unable to swim us back to England even if I had asked it of him! We sallied forth on through your typical small town America, white picket fences, nicely kept wooden houses and lots of lumberjack shirts seemed to be everywhere, and of course those familiar place names again. I motored on through Middlesex and even saw a sign for Guildford. While visiting the town of New Haven, Horris and I stopped for some fuel for the both of us, and then spun on down through Bridgeport heading for the New York state line.

Crossing into NY state I found myself swamped with elation as I had achieved a major goal of the trip, and I'm sure that there would be quite a few nonplussed faces back in Toronto when the news broke that we had made it this far. We carried on along the roadway I had been following, but then made a diminutive blunder by loosing the I-95 when entering the Bronx. By using an excessive amount of driving up and down we finally managed to locate the 95 again, (I was pleased to say without having to stop and ask anyone, this could have been me being a little paranoid though). Having corrected the mistake and while feeling quite self-satisfied with my navigational skills, realisation dawned that I had then missed my turn off for Manhattan and was now heading over the George Washington bridge. Although a slight error had occurred, crossing this splendid bridge more than made up for it. Opened in 1931 the bridge was designed by Othmar Ammann with a width of 120 feet, and a length of 4800 feet stretching out across the Hudson River.

Pulling off the road into Fort Lee I went into a motel and asked a fellow for directions. These he gave me in great detail and sent me on my way, and without even trying to murder me as well! My paranoia was quite relieved! Back across the bridge we cruised, having to pay a $3.00 toll this time for the privilege, and headed into downtown Manhattan, so called after the Algonquian name, an "Island of Hills". After driving around for a while the eyes managed to locate a sign for the Statue of

Liberty, we duly followed the directions and ended up in Battery Park, where upon finding somewhere for Horris to stay, I was charged the extortionate amount of $15 for the privilege! My carriage nice and safe I then headed off to find the queue for the boat out to Liberty Island. On the way I managed to stumble upon a coffee truck selling surprisingly the "Best N Y coffee money can buy". It did, I have to say, go down most splendidly well as the weather by now had turned disagreeably cold. I don't want you to think that my character had turned into somewhat of a lightweight disposition, but the coolness of the climate seemed to be starting to have an effect on me. With my ticket, camera, and a second cup of the "Best NY coffee money could buy" in my hands, I stood in line like the obedient tourist and waited for the ferry to arrive. While standing and shivering we were all fortunately entertained by a couple of acrobats earning their crust on the pavement in front of us. They I believe must have been doing the American version of busking, so when the hat was passed around at the end of the show I happily gave them some money merely for taking my mind off of the bothersome climate. The boat arrived and we all piled on. Everyone then galloped to the front to get the best view of the Statue for the taking of photos. Of course it left no fissure for me to climb into as I had been unaware of this unstated etiquette when standing in the queue, and it also explained why they had all been looking a fraction sly when the boat had docked. So happily not being of a sheep persuasion myself, I sallied to the heel of the boat for the voyage out and took some striking unobstructed photographs of Manhattan, and would then do the contrary on the way back from the island. After a good fifteen minutes at sea we arrived at the base of the Statue of Liberty. It was most impressive indeed. How the immigrants must have felt when they saw the statue for the first time while being processed on Ellis Island before being allowed in to the US, I can only imagine.

Liberty herself was designed by one Frederic-Auguste Bartholdi who chose to make her 151-foot frame from copper sheets attached to an iron framework. The fellow who designed the Eiffel Tower, Mr Gustave Alexandre Eiffel, also devised the framework structure and most intricate his work is too. The edifice was originally put on show in Paris, and upon completion was then dismantled and shipped to America to be finally dedicated in her current position in 1886.

My next obligation was of course to venture within the Lady Liberty's skirt, a trifle forward of me I know as we had only just become acquainted! Under her hemline you are confronted with a long spiral staircase that winds its way to the very top of her crown. At the start of the climb there is a sign on the wall stating that there may be as much as a two-hour wait between beginning your accent and reaching the top during the summer months. She is one lady whose advancing years have not curbed her popularity! I was also most pleased that I had chosen the winter season of the year to visit, as the thought of being cocooned within her robes for a number of hours at the height of summer certainly wouldn't have appealed to my constitution. I worked my way up ascending the tight spiralling stairs to the crown about her head. You are no longer allowed to toil your way through her arm and reach the flaming torch, which was a shame, but nevertheless the view from her forehead looking back across the bay to Manhattan was a most impressive one indeed. The thing that struck me the most was the way that Messieurs Eiffel and Bartholdi had designed and manufactured their statue. Viewing from the interior you can see all the individual copper panels, the way each one had been beaten and riveted, and of course the work would have obviously all been accomplished by hand. This I found to be incredibly impressive.

The first view of the statue that I had commanded, looking out across the water from Battery Park, did draw me into a euphoric feeling. I found though that it was only when inside, looking at the hammer marks in the copper made by those craftsmen of 120 years ago, that I actually felt the soul of the statue. Yes Eiffel did design it, but it was the people who actually built it who are left behind if you look and feel hard enough when climbing up through her cramped, though majestic interior.

The statue is without doubt a monument that is known throughout the world as a symbol of America, and stands sentinel over all that America would profess to be. Although she has Liberty in her name, as I was to discover on my travels, there is a large part of the American population which has no more liberty, or to use its more basic name, freedom, than the people of any other country in the world.

Once I had been thoroughly Libertyed and delivered back to dry land by the ferry, my inquisitiveness chose to carry me for a stroll in the downtown area for a fragment of sightseeing, I determined it best to accomplish on foot as I wanted to make the most out of my expensive $15 parking. My first port of call was Wall Street, or should I say the first place that I stumbled upon was Wall Street. Here I then found the location of the Stock Exchange and walked through the doors to scrutinise the business. The building seemed to be filled with an assortment of fairly conceited people, who obviously believed that tourists such as myself were an unfortunate and unnecessary evil. We were purposefully ushered through a door and then informed that under no circumstances would photos be allowed of the trading floor. Much to my then annoyance my camera was confiscated before I was allowed out onto the glassed in viewing deck. To be honest the view certainly is not the most awe inspiring that I have ever seen. A large number of people screaming at one another, earning and losing fortunes doesn't really inspire a great deal of passion within me. I did seem to be in the minority though, as listening to the conversations of my mostly American fellow gawpers, the people below us on the trading floor were being put on almost god like pedestals.

Having recently come from the Statue of Liberty, the moment again struck a cord with me regarding their culture. Americans seem to have this basic feeling that everyone starts with an equal opportunity to be able to succeed in their life, and that success is defined by money and power. Anything else, perhaps happiness for example, will only follow once you have the first two. Unfortunately life doesn't work that way, and American life is no different to any other in this respect. The opportunities open to some are not there for the use of all the population. The desperate areas of all cities house people who may not be termed by others as "successful", yet the people within them may still be happy, if not totally content with their situation in life. This small detail does seem to be missed by a few people here.

Returning to the pavement I headed up along Broadway for a perusal of the theatres, and to see which of the big shows were playing. The atmosphere as I strolled along was superb, all the people dressed up in their finest outfits, accompanied with the look of excitement and expectation worn across the face before you are about to go in and see a grand performance. Then after the performances, I watched them bustle out onto the pavement discussing their favourite moments and they carried the elated look which people possess having just seen something wonderful and enthralling.

While wandering around I remembered that I had to decide where I would be sleeping during the night. The number of the New York youth hostel was within my pocket, so finding my way to a telephone booth I gave them a call. An answer machine happily replied to my query and enlightened me to the news that the hostel was closed for refurbishment and would be reopening again in three months time.

This news I found to be somewhat of a nuisance, and it also caused a slight obstacle to my intended plans. Immediately I realised that my tired body would be sleeping in Horris again during the night. Thankfully it

wasn't too much of an inconvenience because at least I knew how to as-
semble the seats properly on this occasion. I started to walk back to the
car park where Horris had been left, taking a route which took me around
the rougher areas of the city. I had a strange feeling of being rather conspicuous, the obvious items giving me away as a tourist I determined were
probably the Union jack trousers, matching shirt and also perhaps the
singing of Rule Britannia as I strolled along! Only joking. The dead give-
away was probably the carrying of a camera, even when held discreetly in
hand. The attempted inconspicuous handling of the photographic equipment immediately informs everyone that you're obviously not from these
parts and probably have all of your money hidden about your person. My
defensive paranoia as I thought about these things did again start to raise
its ugly head, but by my sheer bravery and aggressive looks (not really), I
found my way back to Horris, and was very pleased that both he and I
had managed to survive unscathed a day in New York.

I now set out on a motorised tour of the city with my four-wheeled
friend. The first port of call was the Empire State building. Unfortunately
getting a picture of Horris and the whole edifice was impossible, for although stopping outside the door was fine, getting the photograph of the
Morris and building together just couldn't be accomplished because of
the structure's great height. No consideration these town planners! Leaving the Empire State in our wake we motored over the pot holed roads to
the Pan Am building to attempt to secure an image on film of Horris on
the long and famous Park Avenue that leads to the base of the well-
known landmark. Once more I found myself in a state of confusion while
motoring up and down the one-way streets. Left and right we turned in
the vain attempt of trying to find the actual road that I wanted for my
photograph. Eventually I did happily manage to encounter the landmark
that I sought, but unfortunately though not that unexpectedly, from the
wrong side. Even though you cannot see the words "Pan Am" it most
certainly is the Pan Am building in the photo!

Having driven around New York for most of the afternoon, the conclusion came to me that all of the roadways, especially those in Manhattan
are in a most awful condition. Huge holes and drain covers lay like
corpses upon the ground waiting to remove the underside of a Morris
Minor. While attempting to dodge a drain you end up in a hole and when
you miss a hole you hit a drain, frontier type motoring may well be fine
for a big lumbering American car with soft suspension but on poor old
Horris it felt as though the road was endeavouring to tear him apart! Of

course you could not in any way take a dainty approach to driving upon the NY roadways, as by initiating an avoidance of any of the obstacles, you would immediately incur the wrath of one of the innumerable yellow cabs. Experience soon taught me that a combination of horn blowing, lurid vocabulary and rather unkindly gestures were all part and parcel of a taximans day in New York!

My eyes only fell upon a moderately small part of the city during the day's whistle stop tour, but it did bequeath me with a lasting impression. New York is an intensely exciting place where everybody seems to have something to do at an incredibly fast pace. On the streets encountered during my visit, the gentlefolk seemed to mix with the tramps but without ever appearing to realise that they were actually there. Two very distinct parts of society cohabiting during the daytime on the pavements yet come the time when the sun eases its way over the horizon, they both will withdraw to their own highly differing environments. The charged atmosphere, which draws you in to this city, does leave you wanting some more. I am sure it is because of the diversity of the people, and though it is sad to say, it is the inequalities that exist between them that give the city part of its appeal. The other element is in the character of the buildings and of the streets, the fear factor, which as an outsider I felt while strolling about, and it must have added to the overall memory that I took away with me. The feeling may be real or imaginary but it lent a air of excitement to this place which will probably draw me back again in the future.

The succeeding plan of activity was to endeavour to find my way out of town, and of course it was helped by managing to catch the middle of the rush hour. Driving in the rush hour really wasn't the best thing I could have done, especially as it would only help my "getting lost" tendencies which seemed to be turning into a personal vocation at which I was excelling. Coming out of yet another unnamed obscure side street I found myself on the harbour front, right under the bows of an enormous naval battleship USS Intrepid. The sheer scale of the vessel I found quite remarkable especially when compared to Horris's diminutive size. Though being fair, as Horris was designed to carry four people and not 4000, some would say that its not a particularly impartial comparison! Finding myself then by a sheer fluke in the Lincoln tunnel, I noticed signs directed to the I-95 which when found, I hoped would once again head us in a southerly direction. More unmarked roads took us immediately through Jersey City and across into Newark. Here we once again thankfully encountered the I-95, and it was almost like the feeling you experience when unexpectedly stumbling across an old friend, as due to my mornings trepidation of entering New York, the belief had been within me that I possibly would never see anything of this road again.

Driving for about 40 miles to the south of the city, we turned into a huge truck park to get some vital food and coffee, I had chosen well as the car park was so capacious I knew that I would be without problems spending my slumbers there. The only apprehension which came to mind of course, was once I was tucked up in my sleeping bag, of being squashed by one of the enormous eighteen wheeler trucks during the night, though to be honest, by this time I was far too tired to let it worry me too much. The 161 miles that I covered during the day had certainly been the best of the trip so far.

CHAPTER

SIX

A Capitol Day

The morning dawned bright and early again for a travelling morrisman, and I was terribly pleased, to the point of a gleeful smile, that the sleeping arrangements appeared to have been perfected within Horris. Positioning your feet under the dashboard and having your head placed where the rear seat would normally go allowed me to encounter a most pleasant nights sleep. Upon happy reflection, I can safely recount that the evenings slumbers were by far the most comfortable that had been enjoyed so far in the car. (Though to be honest being exhausted may have helped more than a little in this, due in no small part to the lack of sleep from the previous two nights.)!

Examining my large map of the USA the nearest notable location that I had heard of was Washington DC. Using this form of on the spot route planning has, I have found, a great advantage over long previously drawn out plans. The ad hoc method allows you to be completely unconstrained with the locations that you visit, or to put it into layman's terms; a person can lose his way to the point of being bewildered without the slightest worry having to enter his mind. Useful I must say! So pulling out of the truck stop I directed my mount towards the capital leaving only my fond but brief memories of New York behind. I did in fact also leave behind the remains of some donuts that were procured in Manhattan, which I thought was probably a good gesture to the wildlife encompassing the truck stop.

The temperature I was gladdened and relieved to note had increased by about 10 degrees, which made it unnecessary to have to wear every piece of clothing that I owned while motoring in Horris. This also had the advantage of making driving a lot more comfortable, simply because I was not then being restricted outwardly with clothes, and wearing the distended look of the Michelin man.

The heating system that lay within Horris could only be generously de-scribed as fairly humble, though it did work exactly as originally intended. Unfortunately due to a lack of a fan, there was nothing to blow the luke warm air through the heater, so especially when stationary, it took forever to get any reasonable temperature into the car. Any slight increase then in the outside temperature did thankfully make a tremendous difference to a cold Morris Minor driver!

Motoring into Washington my mount and I ended up enjoying the scenic route again, but eventually managed to find the favoured route to our destination, which was the downtown area. Driving about the city streets I then fell in with serendipity, when quite by chance I stumbled upon the White House. Fortune though was not quite at my side because the President had chosen to spend a day away from home. Not taking this as a personal snub, I left behind my calling card with a hand written mes-sage to the effect that I had visited, and was sorry to have missed them.

As far as my photographic opportunities were concerned, obviously, a picture of Horris in front of the White House had to be most diligently strived for, but the roadway turned out to be most popular with vehicles, and boasted a legion of signs saying "No Stopping" which was found to be rather troublesome to the mind. Passing by the end of the grounds the realisation came upon me that a cunning plan would have to be devised for the following day, as the photograph was definitely required for my album. Thankfully all the areas around the monuments in Washington are somewhat open plan, and my luck seemed to be in, as I only had to drive around for about ten minutes before I came across some pleasantly free parking. Horris was then left to spend the day looking across the lake at the Thomas Jefferson Memorial. This I think was a much more suitable and I would almost say, regal parking position for a car of Horris's age and status within society!

With the security systems all activated my feet carried me over the grasslands to visit the various different Smithsonian Museums. Cutting across the park I walked past the Washington monument. The well known obelisk takes the appearance of an enlarged Cleopatra's needle, the likeness of which can be somewhat boringly seen in all the tourist infor-mation that is available for Washington. I decided to defer my visit to the monument for when I returned later in the day.

Veering to my right I now headed down what is known as The Mall, which is the wide avenue of grass with the Smithsonian museums on ei-ther side. It starts at the South end with the Lincoln Memorial and fin-ishes with the US Capitol building half a mile later at the other end. The wide expanse is lined with great majestic trees and scattered about are many a park bench for the use of the families of Washington. I believe that it was the original idea anyway. On the day of my visit they all seemed to be inhabited by over weight men, listening no doubt, to their motivation tapes on personal stereos. These strange characters of men also seemed to be rather red about the face, breathing heavily and discharging a quite disturbing amount of sweat. The dress code of the whole assemblage did appear to be awfully themed as well, track suits and running shoes being de rigueur. Perhaps I should have taken this as a clue to who they all were. When one fellow finally collapsed on the bench next to me I happened to mention the fact that he looked as though he was about to have a heart attack. He replied to me with a wry and sweaty smile "Its OK son I'm a politician, we don't have hearts and besides, jogging is good for me"!

The first part of the Smithsonian on my list to visit was the National Air and Space museum, I had been looking forward to a short sojourn there as space and flight technology is normally rather fascinating and I was not to be disappointed. A number of hours were spent with head crooked back scrutinising the genuine Apollo space ships, the first aircraft to exceed Mack two, the pedal driven Gossamer Albatross, the Wright brothers aircraft and also the Voyager which was flown non stop around the world. Obviously on show within the museum were many other not so famous but none the less still appealing aircraft for the enthusiast to gladly lay his eyes upon. Leaving the Space museum and crossing over the Mall once again, I had to pass through the hoards of death-faced joggers to the National Museum of Natural History. Once again it was found to be very worthy and interesting inside, but unfortunately on this occasion the senses had something with which to compare it to, the Natural History Museum in London. In essence it didn't really compare at all, so after a hasty look around I headed out and walked down to the Capitol building. Built in 1896 the multi columned great domed roof on the top of the building is an extremely impressive and famous sight, the hundreds of steps leading up to the entrance are the pathway to a place of either great freedom or perhaps total corruption. I surmise you have probably noticed a touch of cynicism in that sentence, but there is a belief that any sort of power especially political, will and has, ended up severely testing the integrity of most men.

Turning about face, I now wandered back up the Mall to the Washington Monument to see if it was actually possible to go up inside the structure. Pleasure abounded when it was found that I could A: go up within

it, and B: go up inside it in a lift, as my legs were still complaining somewhat about the stairs which they had been forced to climb in the Statue of
Liberty. Once at the top, delight came over me when finding that the
view was quite outstanding, and as I was the only tourist inside at the
time, I became all the more happy. The four microscopic windows positioned around the top of the monument were enough to give you a wonderful view down on all the sights of Washington. Also reassuringly I
could just about recognise Horris parked where I had left him by the side
of the lake as he was about half the length of all the other cars from my
elevated viewpoint.

My vague touring itinerary now had the Lincoln Memorial at the top
of the page, so exiting Washington's monument I went over and collected
the Morris. We then drove off in the direction of Mr Lincoln to make an
attempt at some good photos. It was with unshakeable confidence that I
thought I was heading in the correct direction for the memorial, but as
some quirk of fate would have it, I wasn't at all! The realisation slowly
dawned on me that somehow I had managed to get on the main highway
out of town, I didn't take this as a particularly bad omen, but having
failed miserably to find Lincoln the first time, I corrected the very slight
navigational error and chose to leave another attempt on the statue for
the following day.

It now became, 'find the youth hostel' time again, and after the problems which had been encountered in Boston I had been hoping for a little
more luck this time. After a half an hour tour of upper Washington DC I
finally came across the hostel about 2 miles from my original starting
point. When entering the fine establishment they told my overjoyed person, that I could place Horris in the underground car park of the hotel on
the other side of the road. When driving in I managed to get chatting to
the car park attendant. He told me how he and his father had owned
Morris Minors back in Ethiopia. He recounted how his family had enjoyed using Morris's because they were such good reliable cars, and he
seemed quite amazed to actually be seeing one again. I believe it almost
bought a tear to his eye. My new friend then decided to expand the conversation and started to sing the praises of DKW cars. This was fine until
we got on to the finer points of DKW wiring looms. As interesting as this
was I had by now been chatting for 45 minutes and was tired and cold, so
I made my excuses, exited left and headed off for the warm hostel and a
hot shower.

A good deal of happy scrubbing later my person was once again clean,
and so I trotted down and flopped out on one of the hostels communal

sofas.   Here I met various travelling folk from Israel, Australia and the UK. Getting chatting to a girl called Lizzie from Cheshire we ended up wandering off to find some food. After an unacceptable amount of walking, desperation finally set in due to a surprising lack of choice, and we had to make do with the highly nutritious cuisine that was offered by the local Burger Bar. I think we would have both normally avoided the foul burgers, but the hostel was at the top of the hill and the frightful food at the bottom, and as no more energy was being made available to either of us until our bodies had taken on some sustenance, the Burger bar had to do. Once we were seated in the bar and had commenced devouring our way through the "lovely" food, I suddenly realised how nice it was that I didn't have to repeat myself every time I spoke for probably the first time in nearly a year.

It had been another most splendid day and we had managed to cover a total 198 miles on wheels, and only what seemed like a few less on foot, so roll on tomorrow!

CHAPTER

SEVEN

Operation White House

Sleeping in a bed, Bliss!!

I have to use the old saying, "That's just what the doctor ordered", because after a few nights slumbers in a Morris Minor, a bed became a real treat.

I woke at half past seven with a vibrant feeling of being completely refreshed coursing its way through my body and was thus ready to do a spot of last minute sightseeing. Retrieving Horris from his under hotel resting place, I loaded him up with my various accoutrements, inspected all of his oil and water levels, pumped up one rear tyre, tightened up a slack front wheel bearing and then we were ready to go. It was at this point that I checked to see how much money I had about my frame, unfortunately my frame could only produce $5.00 So relocking the car I had to go for another walk down the hill to find a bank and cash some travellers checks.

This last minute task completed, we were then really ready to go. My first plan of action for the day was to make another attempt at a photo of Horris in front of the White House. During my stroll on the previous day I had been to take a closer look at the roadway to devise an artful manner of acquiring my picture. About the area I wished to stop were an abundance of signs proclaiming "NO STOPPING" and immense concrete blocks placed on the pavement to stop what I would assume were car bombers. Thankfully as Horris was about half the size of most American cars, you wouldn't really be able to furnish him with a particularly large bomb, so with this in mind I had to obviously assume that the "NO STOPPING" sign couldn't possibly relate to us!

I drove around the block a number of times with the previous days observations at the forefront of my mind, while feeling extremely suspicious and somewhat conspicuous. I had now devised my strategy for the picture, so in true James Bond tradition the hastily concocted plan was set into motion. A number of tall gentleman's strides along the road before the frontage of the White House are a set of traffic lights and positioned before these is a small lay-by where a Morris could pull in. So pausing in the lay-by I waited for the lights to become red. When they chose to change colours we raced out with Horris's poor engine howling, jumped the lights then flew up and screeched to a halt in the perfect photographic position situated between the concrete blocks right in front of the White House. With forethought as my master I had previously set the camera to be ready and primed on the passenger seat for the photograph. Unfortunately due to my heavy application of the brakes when coming to a halt, it had now made its way to a resting place amongst the paraphernalia on the floor. Retrieving the camera was now costing vital seconds and the tension was mounting. Leaping out, I sprinted across the road, focus, focus, snap, pressed the telephoto button (which seemed to take an age to come out), another focus and snap, ran back to Horris (and like all good spies I had left the engine running) then raced off with the mission completed! I'm fairly sure there may have been gunfire heard coming from the local FBI agents as I drove away, but due to the power of the Morris engine I was fortunately able to out run the bullets as none of them hit home!

Operation White House!

I do think that there could be a job for me as a splendid spy as I certainly don't suffer from any sort of nerves! Now feeling rather exalted with my accomplishment, a high powered decision was made to have another attempt on the Lincoln Memorial, meetings were had, plans made, decisions decided, what could possibly go wrong after my previous success?

Sitting in Horris by the side of the road, feeling dejected!

Having made an attempt to carry out my second objective, I found myself distraught, asking how it could have possibly gone so wrong? An overwhelming sense of deja vu started to come over me. Had I been here before? I think that I had, ten years previously to be exact. Having circled Mr Lincoln and seen the three boring sides of the monument, I had become caught up in the flow of the traffic and been swept across the Potomac River to find myself amongst the graves of the Arlington cemetery. The exact same thing had happened when visiting Washington on a family holiday in 1979, though on that occasion I couldn't drive so was deemed quite blameless! Was this purely an uncanny piece of history repeating itself, or was there something on the fourth side of the Memorial that the Americans didn't desire any of my family members to see? Remember, no paranoia here!

I now made what I thought was a honourable retreat, having seen three sides of the Lincoln memorial, TWICE. I felt satisfied. Some might say, and no doubt they will, that the view with Lincoln in the chair is the finest one to observe. Upon reflection though, and being honest with yourself, if you were a starving man and were offered a cake in four pieces, all the pieces the same except one had a cherry on top, would you still not take the three pieces if that were the choice? I rest my case (and possibly sanity!).

It was now time to head out of Washington, the capital I had found to be an engaging city with its friendly people, grand buildings and fascinating museums, but it still had that underlying feeling of being an environment where you either had money or you didn't. Some of the dire areas I passed through seemed so deprived of any social investment, and they were only a stones throw from what is supposedly the home of the most powerful political establishment in the world. There definitely seemed to be something wrong with this picture.

Hopping on to the Interstate 66 that fortune had graced us by starting just by the Arlington Cemetery Horris and I motored out of town. (This by the way is not to be confused with route 66 its much more famous cousin which was to come later). A few miles outside of the city, with

Washington still a reflection in my mirrors, I came across the town of Vienna. Making a moderately shrewd guess I came to the conclusion that it was presumably named after its more famous relative in Austria. Images immediately flashed into my mind of a magazine article I had once seen on an aeroplane I believe, about the Vienna boy choir. The very appearance of these "oh so virtuous" blue eyed, blond haired and sickly pale young boys would be enough to normally make even a strong mans stomach turn. Fortunately I hadn't eaten and had courageously read enough of the story to be reminded of the imagery at this moment. The grotesque thought of there being an American Vienna's boy's choir bought up a rather alarming portrait to my mind. I could see them now standing in the weather boarded church, encircled and entrapped by its white picket fence preventing any means of escape. The priest would be standing over them with hell and damnation in his eyes, striving to cajole the choir into locating some notes to transform into a tune. The choir itself would be made up of a wonderful mixture of descendants coming from many differing races, they would all now be completely Americanised, half would be called "Bo" and the other half "Billy-bob". This would no doubt also cover the female names in the congregation as well! The singing I surmise would stretch to "Old MacDonald had a farm" but probably not much beyond. It would I imagine be the main educational song, because its a reminder to all the singers of their main labour in life, and thus be an encouragement for them to sing all the louder!

Having left Vienna behind with the mental picture and sound of the town still keeping a wry smile on my face, I passed the Manassas national battlefield park where the Confederate forces won two battles in 1861 and 1862. Here of course was once a field of death and horror so my smile was left on the road back to Vienna.

The vicinity I was traversing started to become somewhat hilly. Then all of a sudden, tremendous gradients started to appear from each and every direction, then as quick as a dead bird falling, the elevations turned into mountains, Appalachian Mountains to be precise!

Crossing the river Shenandoah, Horris pulled into Front Royal to be filled up with petrol. Here fully replete we turned left, (or south to be a little bit more precise) and headed down the Interstate 81. It was really an exceptionally nice drive, the mountains about me obviously weren't as immense as the Rockies out in the West, but nonetheless were certainly as fine looking specimens of forest covered mountains as one could wish to see. The poor old Morris wouldn't write any eulogies about the grade at this moment as he was having to give his all on most occasions to get to the top of the long climbs. We had though, come to develop a technique to aid our ascents on the most abrupt parts of the roadway, and it goes by the name of slipstreaming. Allow me to explain. You wait for one of the huge monster lorries to pass on the downside of a mountain and then endeavour to stay with him for the run up the next grade. The best position to place a Morris is, I have discovered, about twenty-five yards behind the thunderous machine. Here you see, the wind conducts itself in a turbulent manner and gyrates back along the vehicle and then has the tendency to actually suck you along to a certain degree. A little bit of extra help does a power of good to an underpowered and overloaded Morris Minor. The difference to your speed if your assistant is able to break away half way up the climb is, I have found to be quite remarkably large.

Having practised the technique to the point of claiming it as a pretty fine art, I felt that if there were a World Championship for the accomplished practitioner, an Englishman would without doubt "raise the trophy", and thus uphold British honour on the roadways of the USA. Motoring on in this fashion Horris and I proceeded onwards through the towns of Harrisonburg and then Staunton, up and down the roadway spinning through the charming valleys and towns of what is a rather rural part of the country. Entering Roanoke my eyes started their evening peruse with the desire of descrying a suitable place to stop for the twilight hours of the day. I was now starting to get a little weary behind the wheel after all the concentration that had been used while remaining behind the lorries. Pulling into a modest garage at a place called Wytheville I immediately realised that I had now certainly entered into "good old boy" country. This presently bought back the jocular predictions that my friends in Toronto had given me before my departure. "Watch your ass " being the main catchphrase. Apparently a young Englishman's "nether regions" in a Morris Minor are not often to be seen in this part of the nation, but as I explained to them at the time "I will be buggered if any good or even bad old boy is going to see my "nether regions" on this trip!" The buggered part of my statement of course caused a great deal of merriment and prophetic type jokes at the moment of telling.

None the less, using caution as my guardian I did eventually manage to depart from the garage with all parts of my anatomy completely intact and unblemished. My sleeping quarters for the night were then found a further ten miles along the road. Lying there in the car ready for some sleep I determined before nodding off to perhaps check the locks one more time, my friends warnings seeming more authentic in the dark! This has been one of the longest days so far on the journey having covered 309 miles, most splendid indeed.

CHAPTER

EIGHT

I'm Cold Now!

Now if I was to let forth a little dirge on the difficulties of Morris travel every now and then, I hope I won't appear to be a person of a disagreeable countenance to the reader, so taking that chance in my hands here goes, "MY GOD, I NEARLY FROZE TO THE POINT OF PNEUMONIA LAST NIGHT!!!" Small lament over, now I shall explain. When I last wrote (worrying about my "nether regions") I had just settled down for some agreeable sleep in what was still a lovely and warm car. I had laid out my body on the nice shag pile carpet with everything in its selected place and actually felt quite comfortable for once as I dozed off to sleep. For not more than an hour did I have my eyes closed in their practised sleeping position when I was noisily awoken by the chattering of my teeth, good gracious it was cold. If any hillbilly had favoured this night to get hold of me, then he would have had to have used a blow-torch and an axe to pass through the ice on the doors, for the temperature was a disheartening amount below freezing during the night both inside and out of the car! Unfortunately the preparations that I had made before leaving in the case of extreme weather conditions were somewhat limited as I had naively assumed that by the time I was this far South the temperature would be quite warm. My lightweight and rather old and cheap summer sleeping bag wasn't particularly helping matters much, leather jackets aren't really known for their warmth and as the only hat that I owned was a wide brimmed Panama, this was perhaps why I was feeling so exceedingly frozen. Dropping in and out of consciousness my whole body seemed to be shaking from the numbing temperature. All my muscles were tensed as I tried to make myself as small as possible to fight off the chill. In an odd way, when confronted with a situation such as this, your mind starts to play tricks on you. When starting to fall into a sleep, shivering thoughts come into your mind "why am I starting to doze, hang on, am I going to wake up from this one, is this the final slumber, I wasn't expecting this for another sixty years". Finally I came to the sensible conclusion that if I stayed in the car for any longer, my personage would probably start to be somewhat troublesome on the "being able to wake up in the morning front". So with this in my shaking mind I climbed out of my burrow and stumbled over to the "rest room". I recalled the last time I had to go into a public loo and sit under a warm air hand dryer to try and make my blood circulate again was in a 36-hour skating marathon I had participated in along the seafront in Southend. At the time I'm sure I remember vowing, "never again will I find myself in this situation"! Well the best laid plans of mice and men didn't take into account the benumbing mountain weather.

The self-inflicted torture by temperature upon my own person (which I am sure would have made the overseer of any dungeon proud) lasted until about five in the morning. At this moment I decided that it was probably the measles you can only catch the once, and not the soon to be received pneumonia. Having had this condition once before and as my arm was also starting to ache from continuously pushing the hot air dryer button every thirty seconds it was now time to start driving again in an attempt to increase my temperature.

I became a hero in my own eyes as even with the cold, I religiously did the morning service on Horris, topping up the engine water and oil in such an expeditious manner I could probably get a job with Mclaren based purely on the time in which I could do these things alone. We moved off with nothing inside of Horris bolted down in the proper place, and with the sleeping bag across my legs in its new use as a blanket. I was just about able to drive out onto the roadway. Half an hour later I felt the tiniest bit more human once again, and this was only due to Horris's little heater having managed to raise the temperature a few degrees above freezing within the atmosphere about my frozen carcass.

We motored off down the I-81 with my still direly numb brain recalling someone telling me to go and have a look at the Smoky Mountains if I had the opportunity. As I was virtually there I had a quick stop to consult the map and plotted the route down the I-40, across route 19 and then right across the mountains on the route 144. This short-lived excursion I wouldn't have missed for anything, my poor friend Horris (who had just saved me from the ravages hypothermia) on the other hand, probably could have done well without it. Many a mile had to be done in third gear, and none too few in second, but merely for the astonishing

views the effort was well worth it. If Horris could speak I'm sure he
would have cursed me that day, many stops were made for photographs,
and the best views always seemed to be at the base of a long hard climb.
I'm extremely glad that I did go to the trouble of replacing the clutch in
Horris before making my departure from Toronto, as all the struggling
starts from the bottom of long mountain roads certainly did test him severely. Of course every action has an equal and opposite reaction as Mr
Einstein proclaimed, so having scaled the top of the mountains, we now
had to come down again! Morris Minor brakes, it has to be said really are
not the greatest and most efficient brakes one could wish to use, which
made our descent all the more interesting. I am most pleased that I used
the slow progress coming up all of the mountains to take the photographs that I wanted, because there was no way I could have stopped to
get any more on the way down!

   After a great deal of scurrilous use of Horris gearbox, and an excessive
amount of two footed brake fade inducing pressure on the centre pedal
to slow us down, we did eventually come out of the other side of the
mountain range to the town of Gatlinburg, and I am extremely happy and
relieved to report, totally unscathed.

   The 441 brought us back on to the I-40 and then almost immediately
to the Tennessee River on which the industrial city of Knoxville has
found its home. My original intention had been to have a stop here, but
as I had recently come through the beauty of the Smoky mountains it did,
in my perception, put it in somewhat of a poor light giving it the appearance of being rather an ill-looking place. I'm sure the city also gave me an
olfactory sensation that was enough to cause displeasure. My obvious
choice then was to carry on motoring through, and head straight for the
next metropolis. Having left Knoxville behind in my mirrors, I favoured a
stopping place about sixty miles east of Nashville. Coming to the conclusion that it wasn't going to get anywhere near as freezing as it had the
previous night, I decided to lay my head down to sleep in the car again
for another night. I only hoped that I wasn't being perhaps a little rash, as
my senses definitely wouldn't appreciate a repeat of the previous experience.

   On another fine day of motoring we had managed to cover 377 severely convoluted and Morris testing miles.

CHAPTER

NINE

Rock 'n' Roll

I awoke to a bright morning and was thankful that I had achieved a most wonderful nights sleep, my general haggard countenance appearing far improved over the previous morns. I am not sure if my improved look was totally due to the temperature staying a judicious amount above 0 degrees on the gauge, or whether or not it was because I was so exhausted from the lack of sleep on the previous night. Whichever didn't particularly matter I reasoned, as I now felt at least a little bit more like a human being and a warmish one at that!

Taking my departure from my nightime resting place, Horris and I motored off towards the world famous country music city of Nashville. Before even a few miles had passed below us I stopped and treated myself to a swift hours breakfast and sojourn in a small family run restaurant prior to going into the city. A couple of days previously I had rashly wasted $3.00 on an emaciated burger breakfast in a fast food establishment that I unfortunately happened upon. With regret I felt that there was probably more nutritional value in the $1.00 bills that I handed over than in the actual food itself, so from now on more prudence was to be taken! Being now a culinary critic I dined to the point of bursting on a veritable feast of a truckers breakfast with as much coffee as I could drink for the tiny sum of only $2.00, splendid! After my feast it took me only about 45minutes of steady driving to get into the downtown area of Nashville. The city had been originally named Nashborough but in 1784 it was changed to its modern title because the inhabitants felt the borough part sounded too British! The local radio companies started to push advertising with music in the 1920's and from here slowly grew the country music industry for which the city is known around the world today. I fortunately had a contact to call during the day, but as it was still quite early in the morning I found myself with some time to kill. Leaving Horris by the side of the road in what I judged to be a safe place I went for a wander around town, and with a stroke of good fortune I happened across a small car museum. Although it had quite a small doorway to pass through as you entered, the interior then opened up Tardis like, into quite a substantial collection of cars. The main theme that was running through the exhibition was of course American vehicles, but managing to ignore these I happened across a few gems. The stagecoach from the opening scenes of the Munster's television programme immediately caught the eye, various Hot Rods from the 50's, and some lovely saloons from before the war. How a nation was able to produce such graceful vehicles before 1940 and then totally lose the plot as far as car design goes from that period onwards is completely beyond me. The one notable "Yank Tank" that was on display which exemplifies this point was the hideous abomination on four wheels, of a Ford Edsel, even the Americans hated this car! Having completed my tour of the museum, I noticed on a table by the door that there was a letter on prominent display. I started to read expecting to find praise about the display from a famous pop star or politician who had once visited as a guest. But no, this most definitely was not the case; the letter was from a lady who had committed the heinous crime of lying. Let me please explain, she had been visiting the museum and had said that her daughter was four and a half years old when in fact she was really five. This unscrupulous act was committed so she could get her daughter in for free. The lady then went on to explain how she was a Christian and couldn't bear to live with herself after this deadliest of sins, and so enclosed her daughter's fee! Yes I am definitely now in the God fearing American Bible belt.

My contact in Nashville was Mike Snow who was a member of the rock and roll band my father played in during the sixties. I had never met Mike before this time, and my dad also hadn't seen him for many a year until spotting him on a music documentary with Alan Whicker a couple of years previously. Inspired by espying an old friend the band members had all managed to get back in touch with one another after a twenty-five year gap.

I called Mike and he kindly invited me over to his family home for the day and also generously invited me to stay the night. Having painstakingly read out some directions for me to locate his house I started to create a mental picture of what he would look like. From his Liverpool accent I imagined him to have a capacious and extremely hairy brown beard, to some extent similar to a summertime Santa! This was rather a wild and unenlightened assumption as I had only ever viewed one picture of him before, and this was of the band in a sixties publicity photo which hangs in my parents hallway to this day. Now as it is hard to recognise even my own parent in this picture, determining what Mike would look like now could be deemed to be entering the realms of difficulty. Locating the house turned out to be rather easy due in no small part to the excellent directions that had been afforded me. Now the driver of the band's old Thames 15hundredweight van had always been my father, so I did wonder if it had been assumed that, like father like son, we were both equally and easily capable of getting lost, which was the reason for the extremely detailed directions I had been given! There was no mention of this theory upon my arrival at the house, but if the assumption had been made, then they had hit the proverbial nail on the head.

When the introductions to Mike and his wife Patti were over, and the traditional welcome of an English cup of tea and biscuits had been polished off, it was most kindly suggested that a tour of Nashville would be the order of the day. Of course I readily agreed to the notion. It was then diplomatically suggested that it would doubtless be better if we drove to the downtown area in the family Chevrolet rather than the Morris. Apparently the reasoning for this was because they were sure I wouldn't like to have to unload all my belongings from Horris to squeeze both Mike and I in!

As Mike earns his living from the music industry by writing songs, the tour of the city had rather a harmonious theme about it, and obviously being Nashville the harmonies were all country and western. We visited all the major recording studios, and Mike's knowledge gave forth on which of the famous country stars had recorded their albums in each of these particular locations. Feeling a touch perplexed I chose not to mention to my escort that I hadn't heard of any of the "famous" people that were being referred to. I only hope that I employed my ooo's and ahh's at the moments that were the most appropriate and judicious so as not to cause offence. My total lack of musical enlightenment it has to be said is not only restricted to the Country and Western genre, I have managed to disperse my skill across most forms of musical styles to the point of becoming most proficiently unaware! It is one vocation that was never inherited from my musically talented forbears though, as my infrequent endeavours at attempting to play instruments have all ended in the resounding riposte that I am most probably tone deaf.

Trundling through town, the Grand Old Opery arose on our horizon, which had me pleased as punch because even I had heard of the Opery, though admittedly I could not lay any claim to an insight of what actually musically occurred within the building. I was justly astonished then to learn that the edifice has not actually been used for about ten years and now lies in a somewhat forsaken condition. The powers of the city have now built a new Grand Old Opery on the other side of town, though this does appear to a historically inclined person as rather a waste of money. I feel the people's taxes would have been much better spent on restoring the original authentic structure.

Having lunch in a blustery but splendid rooftop restaurant I made the acquaintance with one of Mike's friends who was also dining there. He was about thirty I suppose, very tall, with long jet black hair and was wearing about three cows worth of leather in clothing, and his ensemble was finished off with the de rigueur bootlace tie.

It was without surprise I learnt that he was also in the music business as a singer in a country band, the name of which I again chose to feign knowledge so as to help boost the friendly fellow's confidence.

Replete with food we took our bodies off to catch a ferry. I should explain what I mean here, Nashville is bisected by the body of water known as the Cumberland River. Arriving from the east it enters through the suburbs to the centre of town then finds its course out towards the northwest in a fairly meandering fashion. The point at which we were to cross was on the outskirts of town. The ferry consisted of a flat floating pontoon that was able to carry but one car at a time. The local developers obviously couldn't stretch their funds to making a bridge because one side of the river was completely overflowing with shops and modern housing developments, while the other was almost completely untouched by human hand or machine.

After being duly conveyed across the river we immediately found ourselves in pure hillbilly country. I expected at any moment to behold the local cheroot-smoking sheriff giving chase to some good old boys who were trying to escape with a haul of moonshine. I didn't actually see any car chases as normally depicted on Saturday night television, but a number of the dilapidated farms that we passed did, I'm sure, have some stills brewing away somewhere out of sight. I was quite comfortable with the knowledge that it would be only a matter of lingering about a while before some excitement would take place, but as fate would have it, the day of my visit seemed to be the sheriff's day off, so all seemed to be tolerably quiet on the law and order front.

Driving along you could almost sense the history in the landscape, with my imagination sweeping back a hundred or so years to the time of the 1870's when cowboys and gunslingers roamed the countryside. The area we were traversing was the place that the famous outlaw Jessie James hid out in for a long period of his life so I think it would have been a most thrilling time in history to have visited the area to pursue exploration and real unadulterated adventure.

When we returned to Mikes house, his wife and son were there waiting to greet us with a lovely meal already prepared. I unashamedly devoured the delicious food with much glee, as it was the first proper home cooked meal I had eaten since taking my farewells in Toronto. I retired to bed at a fairly early hour to once again make the most of a proper and comfortable bed. I had also previously checked the speedo of Horris to find we had covered the huge distance of 67 miles during the day.

CHAPTER

TEN

The Tacky King

The utter bliss of sleeping on a proper spacious bed for the first time in quite a number of days cannot be properly expressed in words alone. Also the benefit of a really good nights sleep in helping to re-vitalise and re-charge the energy levels in my tired body were really appreciated by this traveller.

With the goodbyes said to my exceptionally genial and hospitable hosts, Horris and I felt the tarmac once again and headed for our day's destination. Of course this had been decided upon in the usual manner of an earnest consultation with the map. Having observed closely the nearest famous locality within a days drive, it was found that the winner was, Memphis. Driving away from Nashville on the I-40 we passed the Kingston Springs. I didn't stop to take in the full flavour of the springs, but my imagination took hold of me in a whirl of religious fervour. I could almost discern the hail and brimstone preacher baptising babies in the full flourish of the natural spring. Being completely enveloped within the Bible belt the spring must, I am sure, be of a somewhat holy persuasion and is obviously an ideal place for groups of credulous believers to congregate.

After motoring on through the town of Buffalo we arrived at, and crossed the Tennessee River, the light shimmering on the water expressing the powerful beauty of nature which can only be captured by the eye. I am sure that a good deal of the local populous would enjoy much better lives looking to nature for their god, or to at least respect it more as an all encompassing natural entity. Jackson is the last main town that was passed through before my arrival in Memphis, so the opportunity was taken to replenish Horris's fuel tank in the local garage. As always, strange looks were given to the car when pulling in and when I went to pay for the fuel the usual questions were forthcoming from the owners and my fellow patrons. It always causes hilarity within my person while waiting for the initial volley of queries to come forth and to then answer in my English accent and use the explanation that we had come all the way from Canada for the sole purpose of visiting their garage!

I arrived in Memphis at about 1 o'clock, and prewarned, had already equipped myself with the great anticipation of ingesting all the "glorious" treats which the home of the "King of rock and roll" Elvis Presley could throw at me. Heading towards the South part of the city I passed the National Civil Rights Museum that is built on the site where Martin Luther King was assassinated. The museum was built to remember the injustice of his death, which is ironic as the City was built to forget the injustice to the Chickasaw people who originally settled this land. I managed to locate Gracelands after a small scenic detour purely to inspect a few of the local industrial estates. The people who drive straight to Elvis's house really don't know what "interesting" sights they miss by taking the direct route.

Leaving Horris nearby, I walked through the gates and up along the driveway to the Mecca of rock and roll fans, "Gracelands". Paying my money I was allowed into the "hallowed grounds" of the house. Immediately I was struck by the time warp that the building had become. I'm used to visiting stately homes and castles in England, which are obviously presented to the public in a condition that reflects how they were hundreds of years ago, and as that is not within the living memory of anyone, it seems a perfectly correct and natural way to be. "Gracelands" on the other hand, is caught in its own time warp. It just happens to be the 1970's and as I can remember at least the latter half of the decade, it feels somewhat strange to be revisiting a part of my own memory. Looking around, all the fittings and designs have the plastic Glam feel of their era, a wide collar and flared trouser kind of decor pervades the whole building in abundance. Although I shouldn't really have expected it to be any different as this was the period in which Elvis died, it does rather seem to overwhelm the visitor with a sense of 70's nostalgia. Strolling about I managed to find myself upon the end of a group starting a guided tour. Reverently following the disciples I entered into a long gallery, which had along either side glass walls, behind which, placed, on mannequins were all of Elvis stage costumes and jewellery. There were only a few of his earlier less extravagant clothes from the 50's and 60's, the majority being once again from the last garish years of his life. The sequinned suits with wing like collars and huge pirate belts simply reminded me of the sad overweight image that he had in my mind before he died. When you see the old videos of his last performances the voice was still there but the fresh sparkle of his youth was but a long distant memory. I suppose if the people who surround you for most of your life always tell you what you want to hear, then you can quite easily fall into the trap of the extreme excess that comes with fame and fortune. The longer this goes on, the fewer people there are around to catch you and tell you when it's time to stop.

Moving about the interior of "Gracelands" and viewing all the different parts of what has become the shrine to Elvis, I couldn't help but overhear the comments of my fellow tourists. The people I have to say were all kinsmen of the badge and "I love Elvis" jacket brigade. Some of the things that they were saying were quite unbelievable, waffling on about how beautiful the decor was, what taste the "King" had, and as for the clothes, when they started to wax lyrical about the style and design of his wardrobe I chose to head outside before my nausea at their sentences was taken as a desecration.

The area of the garden that you could actually walk through was moderately small, and the "keep to the path" signs directed you by stone clad pathways to the family burial plot. Here under silver plaques lay the Presley family. Now all the hype, the lies, the truths and all the words spoken to build the legend mean nothing, they are together again as equals within the ground in which they lay. The one poignant moment that I actually had was here at the graveside. This was probably because I had managed to lose the pack of hero-worshipping tourists along the way. Looking at the eternal flame that burns above Elvis's remains I was pulled in for a moment, in the way almost any flame or fire will do when looked into deeply. The combination of the light from the flame and the sombre surroundings took me to the memory of my own long past family forebears and I found this to be a surprisingly touching moment.

Upon making my departure from Gracelands, I of course realised that there was some unfinished business to take care of, and having suffered the orgy of the plastic Elvis era and his modern day fans, the opportunity could not be passed up. The business to be accomplished was a photo of Horris in front of the famous wall at the gates of the Gracelands estate. Unlike the Wailing Wall in Jerusalem where you do your wailing and then leave a message on a piece of paper tucked into a crack, here once wailing has been completed, you pull out your marker pen and scrawl, graffiti like, the ode for your love of Elvis.

Having checked out the wall on foot, I noticed the area had the obligatory 'No parking or stopping' signs, which seems to be the practise to judicially attach to all surfaces in most parts of America. For the photograph I chose to forget the use of any kind of finesse in my plan, after all I had just spent a couple of hours in a building where finesse was, shall we say, somewhat lacking. So I simply jumped into Horris, drove round to the wall, parked on the pavement, (scattering a few of the anoraks in the process which made me chuckle), jumped out and took my photograph. By the time I had walked back to Horris, the people with the Elvis patches and badges had regrouped by his bonnet with looks of bewilderment evolving across their faces.

Gracelands wondrous wall

As I got in to drive away I gave them, in my best impression of a plumy British accent a "Good afternoon, lovely weather isn't it" before I closed the door. Having viewed their king's final resting place, the emotion of being confronted by a Morris and an Englishman, I'm sure was probably too much for a few of the pilgrims to bear. I imagined them as I drove away leaning against the bar that very night, bewildered with a glass in hand, trying to understand what it was that they had seen.

We drove away from Memphis heading out of town on the I-55. My next main port of call was going to be New Orleans, but the city was going to have to wait until the following day. We motored around 100 miles in a southerly direction away from Memphis before deciding it was time to stop for the night, which was the mileage previously determined to be the minimum amount required to avoid having to hear any more country music! Our distance travelled for the day was 307 thigh-slapping miles, Yee HA !

CHAPTER

ELEVEN

A Bridge to the Horizon

The temperature had been a bit nippy during the night but thankfully I did manage to get a good nights sleep while sprawled across the seats in Horris, and that was even with the sounds of the Jews harp still playing loudly within my mind! Having checked all the fluid levels of the engine in the morning I had one main objective to achieve before anything else, find some breakfast. After driving three miles off the Interstate following signs to a diner I unfortunately found the place closed and boarded up. Usually an occurrence such as this would be taken as being rather lucky, as it had given me the opportunity to see some countryside I would not have otherwise had the pleasure of observing. On this occasion my stomach was jolly hungry so I did rather chastise the world and his children, but most graciously on my part, only for a little while. Then falling straight into the cupped hands of good fortune another diner was spotted which was thankfully open, so with Horris safely parked up, I strolled in. The establishment was your typical small town restaurant, as seen in all the movies that are continually churned out of Hollywood. When pulling up outside of the window I had noticed the waitresses were giving Horris questioning looks in the manner I had long since come to expect, and when passing through the door all eyes were on me. The slight tension pervading the air was immediately broken by the large maternal looking black lady who had me sat down with a much needed cup of coffee in my hands before the words "Morris around America" could pass my lips. Then the whole kitchen of cooks and waitresses proceeded to come out into the diner in an attempt to decipher the way in which I wanted my eggs to be cooked. In the end it was settled that I would have them "sunny side up" and my ravenous belly found this to be most acceptable. After my fry up was polished off, I took a perusal of the menu once again for something that had been seen earlier, and they were called Grits. Again the combined opinion of the staff and by this time all my fellow customers, which included the local policeman, had resolved that I probably would like Grits, so these were served in a bowl on the table before me. Grits as they turned out, seemed to be a cross between porridge and rice, and as it happens was rather nice!

We rolled onwards towards New Orleans in what turned out to be a remarkably nice and warm sunny day. In actual fact it was the kind of weather that I had expected to encounter a lot earlier in the journey, especially once passing to the south of Washington. The distance to New Orleans was, I thought, in the region of 300 miles. Having, already put 100 miles between myself and Memphis the previous night, I realised that it was only a meagre 200 miles further motoring, such had been my haste to get away from the country music! Trundling along in the sunshine during the morning was most pleasant indeed and we stopped in the City of Jackson to refuel and acquire some lunchtime refreshments. When back on the Interstate the time came again to use a driving technique that had first been developed between Albany and Boston. Now remembering that Horris is a left hand drive Morris, I will try and describe the operation as follows. When your right foot and leg has had about as much as it can take resting on the throttle, the numbness having pervaded your whole limb, you hang the said leg and foot around the back of the gearstick and over the edge of the passenger seat outstretched. You can then take your left, (if there were a trade union for legs while driving, the left would certainly be a member) leg and foot and place them in such a way so that the outside of your foot rests on the throttle, and your leg sort of flops sideways. The technique then also gives you the advantage of having a new driving position to play with, because you end up with your back against the driver's door looking out through the passenger window. Of course, safety being an exceptionally important factor, it was found best to still turn your head and look out through the front screen when necessary, though thankfully it didn't hinder in any way ones ability to take in the view from the side of the car. Utilising the afore mentioned system on the long straight roads was found to be rather splendid as they never really seemed to have much bothersome traffic. However, I chose not to try it around town as an attempt to hit the braking pedal in any form of a hurry would, with foresight, be fraught with all sorts of problems, and as we still had a rather long way to go, the plan that safe driving should be the order of the day was chosen.

While trundling along the interstate I came upon a long queue of cars creeping along at a snails pace in the slow lane. Now thinking that this was rather an unusual thing for them to be doing and as I was in my "cruise control" seating position at the time, Horris shot past them all thinking they were purely an assemblage of Sunday drivers. We then discovered the reason for their timid behaviour. There in front of them was a huge black American vehicle straight out of the seventies, with great fins and huge poke you in the eye tail lights, such style! Behind the wheel of this great leviathan was an ancient old lady, so small you could barely see her above the side of the door, and her view above the steering wheel must have been non-existent. It is my belief, that this would explain her driving technique. She was swaying the car from side to side crashing into a small concrete wall (there for some roadwork's) on the hard shoulder, and then swaying back the other way into the fast lane, with enormous sparks as well! My luck was in. At the moment of passing she was engaged in bouncing off the far concrete wall. I cannot imagine what the other road users thought, firstly seeing the madly swerving senior citizen, and to then see me nonchalantly drive past sitting across the front seats looking out of the side window in a 1958 Morris Minor!

After having a thoughtful peruse of the map, the mind elected to take what looked like an interesting detour from the route into New Orleans, so turning off the I-55 and onto the I-12 we headed for the shore of Lake Pontchartrain that borders the city to the North. Then of course I found myself on the wrong side of the lake, but this was the reason for the chosen detour. There is a tremendous causeway that traverses the lake and conducts you, straight as an arrow, across the water into the downtown area of the city. The causeway was in essence an enormously long road but placed up on 30 foot high stilts, and I would believe, using a Morris mileometer as a judge, about 20 miles in length. Following the one straight line of roadway out across the lake you were quite amazingly unable to see anything but the tarmac and the lake beneath stretching out to the horizon. The circumstances made for a somewhat astonishing drive, and what's more the road even had large humps situated within its length so that the bigger ships would be able to pass on through. About halfway across the vast expanse I started to detect a slight, yet still disagreeable misfire from the interior of Horris's engine, also he did worryingly appear to be a fraction down on power. It most certainly wouldn't have been my first choice of a location to have our inaugural breakdown and especially as they had neglected to build a hard shoulder on which a sick Morris could stop.

Thankfully Horris's condition didn't seem to deteriorate any further and we made it safely, though rather slowly across to the other side and into New Orleans. The city surprisingly only has rather a small population of less than 450 thousand and the land on which it was built was originally the home of the Quinapisa and Tangipahoa peoples, who now only make up 0.2 percent of the total inhabitants.

Horris and I motored into the downtown area and found ourselves surrounded by skyscrapers while undertaking a search for the Youth Hostel. Looking about it was a great surprise to me to observe the modernity of the buildings. They were nothing close to what my imagination had expected and it has to be confessed, I was initially quite disappointed. A thought occurred to me that it probably would be advantageous to take a slow glance at the map to perchance help in the search for the Youth hostel which I was having no luck at all in finding. The answer to my quandary then became as clear as a cloudless day. When driving down from the causeway Horris had veered leftwards heading into the new metropolis, whereas we should have favoured the district to my right and driven into, of course, the old town. The error had now been released from its captivity, so with my trusty Morris beneath me, we sallied forth to our destination. The old town was much more as I had expected New Orleans to be, wide boulevards with ramshackle trams clattering down the centre reservation and all surrounded by magnificent lush flowing trees. The buildings were a mixture of modern low storey concrete and the lovely weather-boarded wooden, characteristically French style, mini chateaus all resplendent with balconies and front verandas. The thing that showed itself to be rather strange though was that they did all generally seem to be in a pretty run down state of affairs and with a slight air of decay enfolding the whole district. It is an observation not a criticism, because the wanderer is sure that if all the houses had been gleaming bright and carrying a restored state about them, the area would have lost much of its old world charm. Half an hour after arriving in these Gallic surroundings fortune smiled upon us and we stumbled upon the Youth Hostel. The building did seem to be a fairly dilapidated abode and was nowhere near as clean and prim inside as the Hostel in Washington, but it was a good deal cheaper, so as they say here in the Americas, you gets what you pay for.

Unfortunately during the time that Horris and I had been driving about town while attempting to encounter the evenings sleeping quarters, the earlier misfire had developed into a sort of boom boom noise that ungraciously seemed to be emanating from deep within his motor. A little bit of time was thankfully left in the afternoon before the sun sank beneath the horizon, so mustering some vigour, the hands got stuck in to start on all the prevalent checks to try and expose the problem. Much to my evolving despair, after re-adjusting all the externally adjustable parts, my efforts had succeeded in making precisely no difference whatsoever to the booming noise! As in all situations similar to this, the best option was to immediately have a nice hot cup of tea, followed by a good intellectual drubbing to determine where the problem lay within Horris. After a good deal of speculation the grey matter came to the conclusion that the exhaust valve seats must have started to recess due to the unleaded petrol that I was being compelled to use. The action of the fuel was then of course causing the tappet clearances to close up, thus holding the valves open, which in turn resulted in the vexatious boom boom noise. If you the reader are not at all mechanically minded and have no idea what it was that I have just described, I make no apologies. The process of trying to deduce the reasons for the mechanical problems encountered on the journey did, as it turned out, take on a major role in my travels and as such cannot be honestly left out. My only hope is that the balance though is still in favour of the non-mechanical adventures throughout my writings.

With the judgement made as to where my vehicular problems lay, my groaning regions within now seemed to take priority over, well, everything else. Not being particularly inclined to have to wait my turn in the Hostel kitchen, and not having anything to cook anyway, I withdrew from the building and sauntered off up onto the main road clutching the high expectations of discovering one of the refined Cajun restaurants for which New Orleans is so famous. One hour later with my stomach expressing how it thought that my throat must have been cut, I had to give in and enter a horrible fast emancipated burger bar. The food was plastic along with the cutlery but it did fortunately fill the gap. At the end of the day we had managed to cover 260 miles by car and what seemed a great deal more by foot searching for my dinner!

CHAPTER

TWELVE

The Law of a Fire Route

The power that a good nights sleep can do for you is a wonderful thing it must be said and last night was one of those where I slept like a log. There is some doubt that even the chimes of Big Ben could have woken me from my slumbers. Arising at about 8 o'clock, which on this tour constituted a significant lay in, I felt thoroughly refreshed and once again raring to go with the rising sun. When my departure from the Hostel had been completed the first job of the morning was to adjust Horris's tappets. The result was to hopefully prove my theory of the previous day regarding his strange noises. I of course was rather delighted to find that one of the fellows was to some extent on the tight side, so with glee it was carefully opened up in the hope of curing the problem that had been occurring. Regrettably the tight tappet discovery did not in fact make any difference to the booming noise, so bearing the news well, it was decided that my best option was to leave it as it was for the time being and head off over to the French Quarter and have a stroll about the district.

My original intention before arriving in the city, had been to go for an excursion on one of the famous Mississippi paddle steamers, but everyone to whom I had spoken in the Hostel about my plan had strongly advised me against it. Apparently the trip on the steamer is what you are actually paying to enjoy, as the scenery and views were apparently none too spectacular for a discerning travellers eye. With all these warnings of disappointment ringing in my ears, I ventured down to the foreshore to have a look at the boats, and very lovely and majestic they were too, but the temptation to go for a ride on one was resisted.

A secluded and somewhat hidden parking space on a side street in the French Quarter was discovered for Horris, and so leaving him there I went for my stroll around some of the many Antique shops in the area. One of them had on display a tremendous pair of 1920's nickel-plated headlamps, and for the sale price of only $300. They were certainly worth the money, but even giving it a good deal of thought, regrettably, a way could not be fathomed to pack them into Horris, and the customs men I'm sure would have been maddeningly difficult over them on my flight home. Continuing on my meandering path, a visit was paid to a few of the jazz bars that were in the district. Realisation soon dawned that my entrance was at the wrong time of the day to see any major musical sessions, but none the less all the establishments that I attended had the desired atmosphere and so were found to be both pleasing to the ear and the eye. The time by now had come for me to get a few classic New Orleans and Horris photographs, so collecting him from his side street parking space, I drove around and relinquished the drivers seat outside a typical lovely French Quarter building. At the moment of climbing out of the car a friendly old fellow came up to me and gave me some local wisdom. Apparently if I were to leave Horris in his current position he would without a "shadow of a doubt" be towed away. The reason for this disagreeable news I was advised, was because where Horris had positioned himself was unfortunately, an official fire route. Upon venturing the question as to which road wasn't a fire route, it was pleasantly explained to me that all the roads were used for this purpose, and so no allowance was made for parking anywhere. The feeling came upon me that if they were so worried about space for the fire engines in their streets, would it not be rather sensible for the police and the general populace for that matter, to have smaller sized cars, thus allowing more room for the local fire engines to extinguish all the fires that were obviously breaking out! Of course doing the judicious thing I ignored the fellow's wise message and trotted off up the road to have a study of the few nearby shops before taking the photographs. No more than fifty paces had been trodden when suddenly the urge was felt to turn around and check that my four-wheeled companion wasn't being molested. 180 degrees of rotation later the phrase "oh dear" had to be used as my eyes beheld the local lawman in his ridiculously large patrol car pulling up alongside my machine and giving all the appearances of someone who was about to write a ticket.

So I found myself running down the centre of the roadway carrying a brisk pace, while at the same time remonstrating to the policeman that I was an ignorant tourist from out of town and of course would immediately remove Horris from this irresponsible place of parking. Most policemen the world over feel it is their duty to give patronising lectures, so a quick deflection had the little treat pre-empted, by chattering on about the virtues of a Morris and how they used to be used as police cars in

England. Thankfully the tactic seemed to do the trick as far as me getting a lecture was concerned and more importantly a ticket to take away. As they climbed back aboard their police car I pretended to fiddle about with an imaginary steering lock which of course never existed within the bounds of Morris design. Using these deceptive shenanigans as a time delaying tactic had me feeling quite astute, but unfortunately they must have guessed what game I was up to because they then didn't move off as had been expected. So then with the engine started, I drove around them and slowly motored off up the road, they then pulled out behind me and took the first turning down into a side street. BRAKES!! Now not wishing to be outdone by the local constabulary the gearstick was thrown into reverse and Horris was driven backwards down the street up which we had previously come, neatly slotting straight back into my previous illicit parking position. My arms and legs now stumbled around for the camera, while virtually falling out of the door, and then hot footed it back up the road a little way to take the picture which had originally been desired.

The streets of New Orleans

Carrying a good deal of glee internally and a grin on my face I jumped back in and this time genuinely did leave. As we pulled away it was noticed that the nice fellow who had originally warned me against parking on a fire route was still standing where he had first spoken to me. He had obviously been watching the whole performance, and we exchanged a wry smile when we drove on past.

Discretion being the better part of valour, we then proceeded to hunt out a non-fire route parking meter, and with this discovered, it was fed copiously with the contents of my trouser pocket. With Horris now legally safe under the watchful eye of the loose change taker on a pole, a session of foot walking around the other half of the French Quarter was undertaken. Upon turning down a narrow side street I came across a lone busking saxophone player. At the time the thought occurred to me that he had chosen a tough place to be busking Jazz, as most of his customers would have probably had enough of the style by the time they had reached his particular locale. Now heading off, an abundance of postcards were purchased for me to write upon on the grass of the park that had been passed earlier. Here sitting down in the reasonable sunshine a good relaxed write home was enjoyed.

When eventually returning to Horris, the next, and most important stratagem that had to be undertaken was to choose where my following destination should be, and of course how to get there. Poring over the map in the usual fashion and knowing that we must now head in a westerly direction, it all became quite clear, not so much in a blinding flash, but still bright enough for me to consider the thought of borrowing a guide dog for a few moments! Of course my objective was going to be Houston in Texas and for some extraordinary reason this sounded for the first time, to be a long way away. Driving away from New Orleans I had to admit, that on reflection, my senses hadn't been as impressed with the city as they had expected to be. This was probably due on account of the numerous images that had been fed to me over the years by the film industry, which of course are then rather tough to be rid of when you finally get to explore the real thing.

Heading on westwards towards Houston along the Interstate-10 with the shore of Lake Pontchartrain flowing away to the right, we quite quickly, after about an hour or so, came upon the city of Baton Rouge. The municipality was established in 1719 by the French in a region inhabited by the Houma and Bayou Native American tribes who now barely make up .1 percent of the population. We stopped here to once again refill with the incredibly cheap fuel, and then Horris and I set off, crossing the Mississippi river for what one imagined would probably be the last time on the journey. We were still motoring westward towards Houston when the sensation started to be noticed that Horris appeared to be getting gradually more poorly on the motive power side of things, and after crossing the Atchafalaya river it was also spotted that his water temperature was getting rather too warm for my liking. When we had covered only a few more miles along the road, with a rasping cough and a disgruntled splutter, the motor cried "enough", and turned itself off as if in disgust. We rolled to a downtrodden halt in a cloud of dust on a rather barren piece of unsurfaced hard shoulder, with the huge trucks whistling past my ear and the wind blowing a howling gale across the fields. At the moment of the dust settling it was recalled with irony that it was only the previous day I had spoken to my Aunt and cousin back in Toronto and told them how well Horris had been running.

Having no sparks of any description within the distributor, the coil was changed and various other fiddling about type jobs were carried out to try and find the cure. Thankfully the problem was encountered in only a few revolutions of the hands of my watch, and turned out to be a small piece of wire that had found its way onto the ignition points and was thus earthing them out. The defect located and happily cured, a friendly passer-by suddenly appeared as if by magic, and told me where the nearest garage was to my then position. Fortune had smiled on us, as we had run out of steam only half a mile from the nearest exit from the interstate, so taking the off ramp we pulled into the garage for further investigations. In the more relaxed state of the forecourt where we were now residing, the time was used to change all the insides of the distributor for the spare set that Horris had been carrying for the very purpose. Returning to the roadway the motor did seem to be running in a much cooler state, which pleased me enormously, but unfortunately the booming noise was still there from New Orleans making itself heard like a circling vulture. The sun had now found its way onto the horizon, so I pulled into the next rest area for the night, this way choosing to sleep on the booming problem and hopefully the solution would come up with the sun in the morning. At the end of the days run we had covered 213 miles.

CHAPTER

THIRTEEN

Houston, we have a problem

The morning was started with what you might say was an earnestly positive attitude about my person and having slept on the various vehicle related problems of the previous day, I was now like a race horse in the starting gate, excited with anticipation and extremely fired up to locate the cure. The first hour of the day was thus spent fiddling about in the attempt to find the underlying engine fault that had been plaguing us for the last few days. Time passed and I duly fiddled out of things to fiddle with, then realising it was time for some breakfast we drove on for fifteen minutes and found a nice truckers diner. Unfortunately the fifteen minute drive to my place of nourishment established that my enthusiasm was still no nearer to finding the disagreeable problem, as nothing had changed for the better since the day before.

Thankfully a huge pot of strong coffee and a somewhat unhealthy bacon and eggs breakfast helped to take my mind off the conundrums with the engine. Driving on into Lafayette and pulling over, some more time was spent trying to once again find the increasingly annoying fault. Horris was also beginning to show signs that the quandary with his engine was having a grave power reducing effect on him. Each time we made our way along the road, we ended up going slower and slower. Carrying on motoring with a westward course we fell into what seemed to be a rather stressful routine. It followed something like this. Drive for half an hour, in which time I would convince myself that on this stretch of the road it did feel better, then realise, that no, in fact it was just as bad as before and in actual fact was in all likelihood perhaps a little bit worse. We would then stop on the hard shoulder of the interstate and spend a further half an hour attempting to once again find where the problem lay. Now as the rest of the day progressed in this fashion, it has to be said that the strain of the situation did start to make me maybe a little jaded toward Horris's power source. Trucks whistling past my ear and nearly blowing both Horris and myself clear off the side of the road was not what I thought of as particular fun, and this information was expressed to my charge on several occasions. One positive point was arrived at during the day when we crossed the Sabine River into Texas for the first time. The moment did please me enormously as making it to Texas in my ratty old Morris was, I felt, a minor achievement in itself and also finished off the last few of the contestants, other than myself, in the sweepstakes back in Toronto. Stopping again on the other side of the Texas border in the town of Beaumont as part of our day's annoying routine, we took the opportunity to have a quick look around and a relaxing cup of coffee to help the frayed nerves a little.

To cut a long and repetitive story short we did eventually make it to Houston and thankfully found the Youth hostel without any problems. During the day's travels my fingers had either changed, adjusted or moved everything on the outside of Horris's engine in the hope of finding the cure to the rather bothersome problem that he had developed.

With thinking cap securely placed upon my head I had now come to the conclusion that it was more than likely inside the engine where our troubles lay. By undoing the sparking plugs and removing them from the engine, the motor didn't particularly feel as free as it should be by turning it over with the fan, so the hideous thought had come into my mind that the engine was probably now seizing up. So what could I do? Well the initial plan that was forged was to find a fine vehicle repair establishment, probably outside of the city, where with a fair slice of luck they would be kind enough to allow me to borrow their tools and dismantle Horris's engine to encounter and remedy his problems. It did seem to be somewhat of a rather large inconvenience, but if it had to be done, well then it had to be done, so the scribe below could be a happy one, or one that was written by someone who was in a serious state of exasperation at the vexatious delay. Once Horris had been parked, or should I say left in disgust, outside the Hostel, I went inside and procured myself a bed and something to eat. While consuming my gourmet dinner a conversation struck up with a fellow Englishman called Ted Williams who was also driving around the US. Ted was extremely willing to help in any way that he could. Also, he kindly said that if I did in fact eventually make it to San Francisco, he would probably have a place for me to stay from 17th of December until January. So with my troubles eased a little by the highly recommended method of sharing, the rest of the evening was spent being thoroughly thrashed at chess by a friendly German fellow. Although he couldn't speak any English and I spoke no German, he was sort of a kindred spirit, as his motorbike had also broken down! In the end, the day had been a case of stop and start all the way, but we amazingly still managed to cover 122 miles.

CHAPTER

FOURTEEN

Dismantled Morris

You don't know how much pleasure, let alone relief, it gives me to say that I am once again a happy fellow!

The previous few days had been perhaps a little trying on the person, but with much glee I am now able to say that we had overcome! I'm sure that you, the reader, are dying to know the reason why the mood that pervaded me was such a good one, so here goes.

A fairly restless nights sleep took me through the hours of darkness. The churning over of Horris's ailment in my mind made sure of that, and of course the very real prospect of being stranded in Houston, Texas with a inoperable Morris Minor really didn't aid to much to a restful night either. Upon speaking with a few people in the Youth Hostel the previous night, a small ray of hope did seem to start to appear. The bicycle shop owner's son next door apparently did a lot of work on his own cars and would be around at about ten o'clock during the following day. When the son arrived, I could hopefully borrow some of his tools, (assuming of course that he would let me) and finally fix Horris's problems on the street in front of the hostel.

The morning found me with twiddling thumbs waiting for Clifford as he was named, to turn up at the promised time of ten o'clock. The hour of course passed and so did eleven and also twelve, the conclusion was then arrived at that by this time of the day it would probably be prudent to make a start on the engine without the aid of the non-existent Clifford's tools. Carefully marking all the head stud nuts, and keeping them in order, I slowly undid them all and counted the number of revolutions each nut made, which would enable me to re-tighten them again without the use of a torque-wrench when coming to reassemble the engine. The answer to all my problems sat there and looked up at me when I had removed the cylinder head and had it lying on the ground. Number three exhaust valve had a rather large hole on its edge, and with a degree of annoyance it was remembered as being one of the new ones which had been fitted back in the summer!

Much to my great relief, the valve seat in the head itself wasn't damaged as well, pleasingly all that then needed to be replaced was the valve. Of course, hidden in the depths of the boot I had two old valves which had been sensibly recut on their seats before I had left on my travels, didn't I? Well yes and no, yes there were two valves in the boot, but unfortunately no, the foresight to recut the seats hadn't been accomplished. Oh dear!

Problem: Here I was in Houston Texas needing to find a set of valves for a 1958 Morris minor! The thought of having to spend a week in one place waiting for them to be sent over from the classic British car centre which had previously been found and used in New York, it had to be said, was not found to be all that agreeable. Of course, this was making the huge assumption that they would actually have the valves in stock anyway.

When quandaries such as these make a visit, and finding myself sitting by the side of the road in the middle of Texas with half a Morris engine spread about myself upon a gravelly floor, these are the times that I could call on all the faces of all the people who said I couldn't make it all the way on the journey! Never say die, fight back and prove them all wrong! Keep the energy flowing which didn't allow me to give in, that's what I was there for. Off the feet trotted into the neighbouring bicycle shop, not even mentioning, even by sarcastic means, the non-appearance of the supposed tool bearing Clifford. I proffered many a question about local garages, which helped germinate a legion of blank looks from the staff and patrons alike, but it wasn't until happening to mention how I wished that they had the Yellow Pages here in the USA, that a spark of light appeared at the end of my tunnel. Some sideways glances arose on the ever-helpful staff's faces and would you know it as if by magic, a huge Yellow Pages appeared!

Thumbing through the listings I could feel my heart rate start to increase as a Classic car heading was found, then turning the pages with a pace unbecoming to a civilised person, a page appeared which with hope, could possibly be my saviour. "The British Car Parts Centre". Dialling the number with colossal anticipation, and with everything that I had about me that was crossible crossed, the friendly salesman was spoken too. Blow me down, was the joyous expression used. They only had a valve!!!!! My joy, relief and happiness were now unconfined, and making my dash back out through the cycle shop I left in my wake a whole pannier of thanks to the staff, for their patience and for the page of the Yellow book which was now clasped within my hand. It now became prudent to carefully study my street plan of Houston. It appeared that there were about twenty miles between my new valves and Horris's kerbside abode, so using my aversion to public transport as an agreeable excuse, there was obviously only one course of action to take. Immediately I started to reassemble all the parts that were spread before me on the ground. This even included (much to any engineers distaste) all of the distraught pieces that had previously been removed. Horris then popped and banged on our journey over to the other side of town to find and greet with open arms our splendid new valves!

We finally pulled into our saviour's abode at 3 o'clock which in my opinion was rather good going considering the amount of work I had managed to get through up to that moment of the day. Here before me was a fairly large and neat workshop and a big (thankfully) storeroom all set within a high wire fence surrounding the premises. My eager person was happily now offered the chance to restock with all parts which recent experiences had taught me I may later need, and of course the priority was given to some valves and also a spare head gasket set, but only for good measure! The exceedingly friendly and helpful owners kindly allowed me to do the necessary work on Horris in their carpark, once more the cylinder head came off, all the valves were taken out, and I determined that a quick session of valve lapping for them all also wouldn't go amiss. Of course one had to now again call upon my new acquaintances for assistance, as my toolkit didn't have any lapping paste or even a lapping stick within its environs, but true to form they came up trumps with the required items. By 5 o'clock it was dark, but thankfully all the valves had been lapped in and all that remained to be done by this time was for the valves and their accoutrements to be cleaned and reassembled to have us once more on our way. This however, I wisely chose, could wait for the morning as the sky was now quite dark, and tiredness had caught me up. The grubby appearance which my frame wore was washed away in the garage's cloakroom and I was even kindly offered a shower at the home of one of the chaps if I would like it, but with graciousness in my voice, it was turned down. All that was really wanted then was to lay my head down, drift off into a deep sleep, and dream away the day's escapades.

Sometimes it can be rather difficult to judge a situation when it occurs and of course when passing judgement on someone, it is most prudent to take great care with your thoughts, but when self preservation may possibly be at stake it is best to be cautious. The thought had sprung to mind during the day. While beavering away on Horris, one of centre's customers had turned up in an MG. He was a fellow of about 55 years of age wearing a rather expensive suit with a yellow rose in the lapel and a big cravat under his chin. He walked with a bit of a skip in his step and also wetted and then stroked his eyebrows on a number of occasions! He was an extremely pleasant fellow and seemed most interested in my journey from Toronto to Houston. When he heard of my predicament and realised that I would be spending the night sleeping in the car, he became remarkably insistent that I should stay with him in his "Huge" apartment for the night. Although feeling guilty thinking it, my mind was rather suspicious of his real intentions, so with regret in my voice the kind offer was obviously turned down. If a misjudgement did occur at that moment I can only apologise, but it wasn't the type of wager that this particular Morris driver was willing to take. The weather during the day had been most strange, after all the unexpected winter cold, the sun had shone all day long and the temperature had pleasingly stayed in the 80's from sun up to sundown. It was what had been expected by the time our journey had reached this far south and especially by the time we had arrived in Texas. With the adventures of the day by then happily behind us, when checking the speedo I was gratified to discover that we had covered the sum total of an incredible 13 miles!

CHAPTER

FIFTEEN

Shuttle Diplomacy

I was up with the larks in the morning, or at least up with their US cousins. Of course, it was for the sole purpose of getting straight back to work on the reassembly of Horris. A comment must be made about the surprise felt when a huge thunder-storm chose to pay us a visit in the early hours of the morning, and only moments after rising from my slumbers as well. My previous notions believed that it never actually rained in Texas so the precipitation came as somewhat of a surprise to this particular traveller. Another thing that my eyes were also finding most strange in this State was how green all the countryside appeared to be. My image of Texas before arriving here had always been of vast deserts and huge rocks. It only proves how wrong you can be.

After a good deal of hasty spanner work, my eyes glanced at my watch and noted that it was only 10.30am, and we were thankfully once again up and running. The news dissolved me into one seriously happy fellow, with a high degree of splendidness exuding from my person.

With an unprecedented amount of thanks given to the chaps in the classic car shop, and another spare valve acquired for the "just in case" scenario, we were once again on our way. Now is the time to admit that after stroking the pages of the map on that rainy morning, the temptation had been there to head straight for Dallas. The process that had to be gone through was in a way to convince myself that the trip was definitely back on. The stopping off in Houston was for the sole purpose of seeing the NASA space centre, so with thoughts of Dallas placed firmly in the back seat; we motored off in the direction of the space park.

Taking the now sweetly running Morris off up some side roads, we had in our sights the quest to find NASA, so portraying the Grand Old Duke of York, in a lost fashion, we came straight back down the side roads again! Surprisingly though, in only about half an hour we found ourselves parked amongst the wallowing American vehicles and great yellow school buses of the NASA public carpark. The whole complex was situated on a vast area of land that seemed to be spreading out in all directions with little inhibition. I then started on what seemed like a walk of possibly three or perhaps even four miles to reach the visitors centre, where my aching feet eventually delivered me. Here, time was spent exploring all of the different displays and absorbing reams of information about space travel, but knowing all the time that I had to focus on the main purpose of the visit, which was to see the space shuttle in all its fascinating glory. With enough knowledge of spacecraft absorbed, I strode off following the firmly conspicuous signs along a winding path towards my goal. They directed me through all of the large buildings that made up the complex, and after a while a pattern started to emerge. It seemed that once you had reached a certain point, or in actual fact a certain corner of yet another vast hanger, your signposted trajectory turned you through 90 degrees and directed you off down yet another long pathway taking you virtually into the sunset itself. After an age and a half had passed, at the moment when I began to think that I should have bought some provisions and a compass with me, finally the shuttle hanger chose to appear.

Upon entering the hanger it was found with real disappointment, that the genuine shuttle was apparently away on business, so my expectations would have to make do with a wooden life size mock up that they used for training. It was in fact, still a most splendid exhibit, and what's more, I had it all to myself, which made up for the wooden shuttle not being the real thing. Behaving in a youthful fashion my person was able to climb and play all over the exhibit, twiddling knobs and pulling levers to my heart's content. My inhibitions found new freedom as I explored this child's paradise, and found myself gushing joy that I was probably more than likely there on my own. It was easily surmised that most people would have probably given up on the protracted trudge that was needed to find the shuttle hanger in the first place, so there were no complaints on my part about the woodenness of the exhibit. After becoming all hot and bothered by being a spaceman for half an hour, I trotted over to the Luna Lab which was thankfully quite close, and entered through an air lock and into the Lab itself, though this may have been merely a tourist gimmick. The lab was found to be most engaging; a good deal of moon rock and moon dirt, (though I suppose that they had both been one in the same thing at some stage of their life) and other moon related paraphernalia were housed within its environs. We had the video playing of the actual landing on the moon surface, which of course, you really can't help being transfixed by each and every time that it's shown before you. The space suits from the landing were on display as well. From their bulky size its a wonder that the astronauts were ever able to stand up, let alone have the energy to jump about as seen on the film, perhaps the weightlessness had something to do with it!

Now the signs that they made me follow on the way to the shuttle hanger had dire warnings about not leaving the official pathway. This was under the penalty of being used in the next dangerous space experiment. I suppose it is to make sure that the humble traveller doesn't stray off into a "secret" area and spot something of great importance. The long walk was all well and good on the trek out to my destination, but once enlightened to their zig zag route planning there was no way that I was going to go back by the way of their signposts. Taking the decision quite easily, my striding posture quickly fell into the Roman theory of road building for my route back to Horris, which simply meant, a straight line! Off I set at a brisk pace using the huge rocket in the carpark as my bearing, striding onward with my head held high pretending I was supposed to be where I was, and that I knew exactly where I was going. The technique lasted for a splendid ten minutes when all of a sudden a fellow in a suit and lapel badge accosted me with words to the effect of "what the hell are you doing here?" On this occasion I thought it prudent to probably not use the Roman road makers form of negotiation, i.e. a swift sword in the chest, a: because it would make an awful mess on their nice grass, b: I also wouldn't like to have to pay his dry cleaning bill, and finally and most importantly c: I had left my sword in England!

With my tail dragging between my legs, the over serious suit escorted me back to the official path and once more I was on my way, I chuckled with each step that was taken though as I had probably still saved a good fifteen minutes on my return journey by using the short cut. For all the fuss that the suit had made, I'm sure I didn't see any secret rockets or aliens from crashed spacecraft wandering about. Perhaps if more attention had been paid in the "how to be a spy in a foreign land" classes while at school I would have had better luck!

When first arriving at the space centre, Horris had been left parked near the famous gigantic rocket that lies on its side in the field on the other side of the main road into the complex. Now this really was an impressive site, the sheer magnitude of the thing was awe-inspiring. The structure had been separated into a number of sections so you could observe the different internal booster rockets for the separate stages of its flight into space. Walking around the incredible creation you couldn't help but get a feeling of the sense of sheer power and fury that it must have produced in its heyday while on its flight to the moon. A rather poignant thing happened when walking back along the rocket's far side. Some birds had obviously chosen the interior of one of the chambers as their favoured nesting site, and upon hearing the noise of my footsteps they all flew out in a most startled manner as I passed on by. The contrast between the assumed incredible technology that man had used to get this mammoth of steel in the air, and that of the natural flight of the birds I found to be quite humbling.

The next stage of my days plotting was about to come into effect. Of course it was "Horris photograph time"! The best picture that could be thought of would be of the car in front of the space shuttle on the runway to the launch site. As I had already unfortunately discovered, the real shuttle was away on a mission in space at the time of my visit so this idea was rather out of the question. The alternative of using the mock up shuttle that had previously been visited seemed to me to be quite acceptable though. A quick trot back to the visitors centre to enquire if it would be possible for me to drive round into the shuttles hanger was received by, I have to say, a combined look of contempt and horror by the staff and their associates. Finding myself most dissatisfied and surprised with the unexpected outcome of my request I strode, with a defiant purpose in my step, back to the carpark. Upon reaching my four-wheeled accomplice, a new plan had already been concocted within the grey cells above.

My impending triumph was to simply use the huge lunar rocket that had so impressed me earlier, as the backdrop for my photo. The only likely place of access that could be found after several minutes of scouting about was from the rear end of the spacecraft near to where the carpark was situated. Even here though as a protective measure, they had laid out huge concrete slabs to prevent cars driving up too close to the spacecraft. The obvious mistake that their generals had made to a British eye was to leave a gap between each consecutive slab of concrete in the defences. The blunder was a grave tactical error on their part. You see, they had used the average girth of their own gargantuan cars for the width of the gaps between the barriers, a direly nonsensical oversight for a superpower to make I thought! So with Horris fired up, and of course still purring beautifully with his new valves, we moved up in a quite innocent looking fashion to the battlements, and then like a great Trojan Morris, gracefully squeezed through the gap, almost as though it had be especially designed for us by an undercover Englishman working for NASA in years gone by! Once through and aligned for the picture I sauntered backwards to the required position and took my lustrous photograph.

The mission accomplished, it was then noticed that one of the giant yellow school buses were beaming at me with forty pairs of youthful eyes, which obviously had been watching my every move during the manoeuvres. Although they were not aware of my nationality, I chose to give them a little bow for my performance in the hope that they would recognise a Englishman when they saw one and that this would in turn help perpetuate the splendid image of our country. Motoring through the slabs on my return, a goodly amount of satisfaction came over me as another objective had been successfully accomplished. It of course became especially gratifying as I recounted to myself that only a few days previously it had been looking as though Horris was on his last legs. I always find it amazing how over the course of just a day or even a few hours the situation that you find yourself in can change so dramatically for the better. Sometimes it's almost merely a case of waiting for it to happen because you know it will.

With the space centre operation completed it was now time to once again consult the map for the next stage of the journey. Laying the charts out across my legs the pin fell into Dallas, so turning north we drove onto the I-45 and started on our way. Trundling along, Horris was running most sweetly which pleased me no end. Passing to the right of the very pretty Lake Conroe we stopped in Huntsville to refuel both the car and myself; with this completed we set off again passing through Madisonville and another Buffalo, the latter one I have to say bearing no resemblance to the Buffalo which was met on my entry into the States. With eyelids becoming heavy it was resolved to stop for the night about seventy miles from Dallas, as some New Zealand fellows I had met in the hostel in Houston had informed me that there were no beds at the Inn (the Inn or Hostel being closed) in Dallas. Once again it was a service station carpark for us on that night. We had contrived to cover 216 miles during the day including the exciting shenanigans round some spacecraft.

CHAPTER

SIXTEEN

Who put those gates there?

The particular week of the year in which I am travelling must have been destined at my birth to be forever known as bother week for me. Why you ask? Was not my loyal friend running "most sweetly" yesterday? Yes he was, and still was when his front wheels touched the tarmac first thing in the morning. I had motored off down the road in a none too brisk fashion with the intention of stopping fairly quickly for some breakfast. Fifteen minutes later daa, daa, cough, cough, splutter, splutter and I found myself to be the owner of one remarkably badly running Morris! Noooooooooo! Not again, not so soon, echoed across the land!

Pulling off the road at various points in an attempt to remedy the problem proved to be fruitless, and annoyingly to add insult to injury it had now decided to snow, and this was in Texas as well! Once an hour had passed of this stop, start procedure, I once again pulled off of the interstate. Horris and I found ourselves on what appeared to be a short dirt road that swept down from the I-45, taking a turn under it and then reappearing back up the other side. Presumably the underpass would normally used by the local police force for a quick U turn when they needed to chase some local wrongdoers. A small peal of irony passed through me while thinking that it would lay quite well with my day's luck to have a major chase come through the tiny subway while we inhabited it. The image in my mind of them all (wrongdoers and police) having to virtually stop and squeeze past me before resuming their chase, did, I have to admit bring a grin to my face. Parked directly under the I-45, a command exuded from me with a stern cut to my voice, in the direction of Horris, to the effect that we were not moving on until the problem had been found. Even if it meant that we both were going to starve under the roadway, we were going nowhere! My dissection started with the ignition, swapping, changing and adjusting all sorts of things but to no avail. Mov-

ing on to the carburettor and attacking it with gusto, I once again adjusted, moved, pushed, pulled, shouted at and checked the whole induc-
tion system but again with no change in the patient's condition. While sitting on the floor leaning against the buttress of the road above, eating between sighs of desperation, a Mars bar that I had intended to save for my
supper, a small glimmer of a thought appeared between my ears.

Before setting off on the journey I had procured a new ignition coil as
a back up in case of breakdown. So when the problems with the valves
had started to appear not long after New Orleans it had been fitted as a
possible remedy. As for the old coil, it was still laying in the boot amongst
my spares, and by now was looking rather dejected. Surely this couldn't
be the problem with the motor, after all, it was a brand new coil sitting
there on the engine. If I went ahead and changed it back for the old one
and there was no change again, I might feel like getting perhaps a trifle
irate. The Mars bar was now long gone from this world, and as much as I
tried, my mind really couldn't think of anything else to check, so a coil
swap it was to be.

As my arm pulled back and gave an almighty throw, the sort of throw
that my Canadian tutors had taught me that baseball pitchers use during
their complicated game over here on this side of the Atlantic, the "new"
coil came to its final resting place, and finished its long journey from
China badly dented against the concrete of the underpass I had spent the
past hour and a half inhabiting.

We pulled back onto the I-45 with the thirty year old British Lucas coil
once more back in the position it had probably held since Horris was
new, now purring like the finest Swiss watch that I had come to know
and to befriend. Motoring onwards, a gleaming city appeared on the horizon. As we grew closer I knew that the place would embody my image of
the USA.

Dallas was originally founded in 1841, as a trading post on the Trinity
River by one John Neely Bryan and previous to that time had been the
home of the native Anadarko people. The city found international, but
unwanted, fame when John F Kennedy was assassinated while passing
through Dealey Plaza in his Presidential cavalcade. More recently the TV
series "Dallas" of the 1980's gave the metropolis worldwide fame as the
home of scheming and corrupt oil barons. Arriving in the downtown
area, I found the grand design of the skyscraper buildings to be positively
beautiful to my none too discerning eye. In the past, my senses had never
particularly found skyscrapers to be all that engrossing when placed in the
vicinity of older buildings, but here in the Dallas municipality it was pure

skyscraper architecture gone mad. The immense gleaming mirror clad structures had me roaming about with my neck craned upwards. They even had buildings with holes in them for the purpose of amusing the strolling traveller, no doubt. A good amount of time was spent walking the streets between the edifices of Dallas, purely marvelling at the architecture before me. It reminded me of one of the great car shows where the manufactures let their designers have a free rein and build the concept cars of their dreams, but here they seemed to have built concept buildings, and were actually using them.

My next port of call on famous Dallas sights was an obvious one really. The TV show, which was the namesake of the city, was based at Southfork Ranch. A knowledgeable fellow at the hostel in Houston had advised me that the ranch was in a place called Plano to the north of the city. As I said to him at the time, the name Plano didn't seem to particularly fit with the image of the show witnessed by myself on the TV during my youth, so perhaps this is why it was never mentioned. Driving for about thirty miles away from the city Horris and I found Plano, again not quite the short drive that we were all led to believe on the show. A sceptic could almost start to believe that the series was purely a piece of fiction! Finally we found Southfork after quite some driving about and getting lost, and this was only because I asked some bored attendants in a garage for directions. Motoring down a side road following lots of other tourists in their cars and vans (you can tell that they aren't locals by the number plates) we came upon the famous view from the end of the drive. Pulling off the road, it immediately became apparent that I was the only one who was stopping. All the cars and campervans were slowing down as they passed the gates, making a slow and respectful drive past as though someone had died and was lying in state. My sides nearly split while observing their hilarious antics, why were these people showing such respect to something that was essentially unreal and pure fiction. At Elvis' graveside it didn't happen, the people there were as brash and loud as I had come to expect of Americans, so why here? I suppose the TV show had been such a phenomenal success with the people of this land and of the world, that all the trials and tribulations that had gone on in the programme had somehow appeared real. It must have etched itself to such an extent on the life cycle of these visiting tourists making them in some way believe it was fact and so they then felt they had to show such enormous respect.

I don't know if it was spoiling their perception of the place in any way, and it certainly didn't seem to be, but completely adjacent to the ranch is a huge tower type construction with a small amusement park at its base. The park is the reason why all the camera shots that you ever saw from the end of the driveway were from the left three quarter view, to purely miss the ugly neighbours. You would have thought that JR would have picked a quieter spot! Horris and I pulled out of our parking place with some difficulty as all the slow moving gawpers were getting rather in the way and then crossed the road onto the end of the Southfork driveway. Trying to open the gates to the ranch met with failure as the owners had rather inconsiderately chosen to lock them, so unfortunately a picture was out of the question in front of the house as there seemed to be no other way in, having already checked out a wall and ditch that surrounded the property. Not to worry though, as a good photograph of the car backed up against the gates would more than suffice, and I only had to turn Horris around as he was facing the wrong way for the picture. Now the problem with reversing a Morris which is full of a years worth of accumulated junk and also is not fitted with wing mirrors, is that you simply cannot see where you are going while reversing. All my tooing and fro-ing was making an agreeable performance for the people passing by, but the final act though I think did really steal the show. With Horris nearly aligned in his designated position, it was just a case of once again reversing a little to the desired photographic spot. The reversing side of the manoeuvre went most splendidly well without any problems at all, but just at the crucial moment I was somehow distracted and there was a big crunch! I had reversed into the gates of Southfork Ranch, Wonderful!! The bounce off the gates moved Horris forward a bit so I thought perhaps I ought to hurry up with my photo as the security camera was now looking at me with disdain, and also a disagreeable looking golf trolley filled with security guards was now heading down the drive in our direction.

Southforks dented gates!

Photograph taken and we were off, yet for all our work at our performance, no ovation was forthcoming from the passing crowds!

Heading now across country for a little while, we passed the aptly named Lake Dallas and got on to the I-35 leading north towards Oklahoma City. The border between the state of Texas and Oklahoma is divided by the Red river which must be one of the most squiggley borders in the whole of the US as most of them normally come from the "straight as an arrow" school of border design. Motoring onwards for quite a few miles we eventually came to a stop and I treated myself to a motel room for the night as the weather forecast was for freezing temperatures with the possibility of snow during the night. As I had no intention of trying to catch pneumonia for the second time in my life, I felt most content with this choice. Sitting in the piping hot bath with all the complimentary paraphernalia that they leave you in motels thrown in for good measure, I looked back in my minds eye on the journey so far. Thinking back along the roadways of America I had partaken in a thoroughly enjoyable and somewhat adventurous passage to this point. Even all the breakdowns became important in the bigger picture as overcoming them lent a certain spirit to the whole thing. As we were now about halfway across the country, the feeling, sitting there looking like a lobster was that the second half of the trip would be as enjoyable as the first, and with a little care and luck, I wished that no further disagreeable predicaments would happen to either Horris or myself in the future miles. Talking of miles we were now about five miles south of Oklahoma City with a total of 286 miles covered in total during the day.

CHAPTER

SEVENTEEN

Dodgy Navigation

A combination of my long hot soak and a wonderful deep sleep did me the power of good during my long noontide slumbers. It has to be said that my person most unquestionably needed it, as all the tensions and stresses that had been procured during the recent breakdowns purely floated away in the night. The intention had been to make an early start in the morning, but due to the room being fitted with overly thick curtains, which of course were closed, I didn't realise that the sun had shown its face above the horizon until 9 o'clock. All the same though a good deal of appreciation was felt from within for the lay in.

With all my gear re-loaded into Horris my feet carried me off to find the free donuts and coffee that seem to come with most motel rooms in the States. Upon finding their location, one has to admit to having consumed a large number of the highly sugared delights almost to bursting point, as they were rather lovely. Now it's not that I am in any way a greedy person but a discerning summary of the Motel rules was taken and it was noticed that they did use the word "donuts" in the plural to describe the guest's allowances in the mornings. With self-righteousness in my mind to help ease my guilty conscience, my person was found sitting next to the tray containing the objects of my desire with an open bag at my feet. Each time the lady that was behind the counter, who also was in full view of my mischief, turned away or looked down to her paper, one more donut was helped to escape from its table top penitentiary. When the bag had reached its donut capacity I did a surreptitious and seriously cool walk back out to where Horris was parked. Climbing aboard the realisation came over me that the life of a donut thief wasn't really for me, as although it was quite cold outside the sweat was pouring from me like a pig on his way to market. It was at this moment that the realisation came over me that the key to my room still lurked within my pocket. Oh no, I had to go back inside and face the lady! With trembling steps and visions of being locked up in a hot and sweaty gulag somewhere in the backwaters of Oklahoma my feet tip-toed back inside, praying like a mad thing that she had left her perch at the counter. Unfortunately not, she was still there as I approached and when handing over the key asked me if I had enjoyed my breakfast! Gulp! Was she now trying to catch me out with the old moteliers ploy of being direct and to the point? My mind wasn't sure, so coming back at her with a bold and confident "yes" seemed appropriate. It was bold and confident when the signal was sent, but when the command actually reached my vocal cords even I could barely hear it, so a second attempt was executed, this time with a little more volume, while finding myself backing out of the door.

I had chosen the day's objective the previous evening. With a goodly amount of glee, the finger had fallen on Dodge City, which was a location I had always wanted to visit, as it was where the famous gunfight at the OK Corral had taken place. Studying the map for a while, the eyes noticed that there didn't seem to be any direct route that went straight to Dodge. It meant we would have to head off the beaten track and go across country on the side roads for a change. I knew full well that it would be taking rather a chance by driving this route, simply because all the recent problems with the engine made the thought of being stuck out in the complete middle of nowhere not all that appealing to the old constitution. But thinking it through, a "what the hell" came to mind, "I'm probably only going to come here once", so the gamble was to be taken and a drive into the sticks was set.

Horris motored on through Oklahoma City and although we didn't stop and spend any time there to make a particularly detailed analysis of the locale, I did come to the following concise synopsis upon driving out of the city limits. The appearance given to me was that the city was struggling to keep up with its more illustrious neighbours, but giving off a most run down and sullied presentation to the passing traveller. My belief is that this state of affairs can happen in any country and it certainly does in England. It appears that the social amenities, aka, keeping the place clean, are left as rather an afterthought by the local councils who prefer to spend their allowed budget on what are perceived to be more important things. The problem with the method described is that the population then have very little love for the place in which they live, which then goes on to breed an apathy amongst them for taking care of their local environment. From the former I don't mean so much the natural environment, though any help to stop polluting nature is obviously good, but more simple things like not littering the place, and having piles of debris outside of the buildings. Be you rich or poor, you are capable of putting rubbish in a bin rather than on the floor and if more of the local money was spent on at least trying to make a city look reasonably nice, it would I'm sure make a start at lighting the touch paper of wealth and prosperity. It may seem a rather simplistic view to take, but having pride in where you live I'm sure, would make all the difference. Oklahoma city did start me off on these thoughts, probably because of the glaring contrast with Dallas through which I had previously passed and really admired. Of course you can say the same about many other cities and areas of the world, it was simply that it came into my mind at that particular moment and was nothing personal against Oklahoma.

Our wheels turned onwards until we pulled off and stopped in Watonga City to acquire some more fuel and engage with a cup of coffee in a small local diner. The usual conversation was had along the lines of "where you'll from son" and as I was now more off the tourist trail, they seemed increasingly curious of my little journey and the mode of transport I had chosen to complete it in.

A goodly amount of miles further along the road from Watonga our path crossed into the state of Kansas and from here the countryside seemed to immediately change. The vast undulating plains that I remember from many a cowboy film produced by Hollywood over the years hove into view on the horizon. The old saying about "there being Indians in them thar hills" could well have been said here for the first time, as you could well imagine tribes of native Americans and herds of Buffalo roaming these grasslands in years gone by. The side roads upon which we were now travelling, I felt, would probably make a Roman road builder weep with tears of pride if he were to see them. They head off to the horizon keeping a dead straight line with never a curve or even a bend ever being encountered. I noted seeing on several occasions' birds that carried the demeanour of small eagles, or at least possibly large falcons, sitting on the telegraph poles that run inexorably alongside the roadway. With my camera in hand, clutched in anticipation for the next encounter with one of these glorious feathered creatures, I drove along the nature trail with baited breath waiting for the inevitable encounter.

Seeing a rather agreeable example perched upon his chosen position atop a pole further along the road, I slowed down and stopped Horris in a hushed and unobtrusive manner about twenty five yards before his station. I'm sure he hadn't noticed me which I felt was rather splendid, so by darting between bushes was able to prowl up to his pole and capture a

couple of good shots on my camera before he realised he was being observed by this amateur naturalist. Woefully the noise of the camera gave
him a start from his daydream of tasty dormice and shrews, and he took
off in a skyward direction no doubt cursing his own lack of attention, I
feel that the true identity of my feathered friend will more than likely
cause a deal of discussion when the slides are eventually shown!

Our tracks finally led us into Dodge City at about three o'clock in the
afternoon after what seemed like an eternally long drive. Of course, in the
back of my mind I knew that it was well worth making the big cross
country detour, for I was about set my eyes upon the very location where
the infamous Gunfight at the OK Corral had taken place. When driving
into the city I did feel that the city elders were not capitalising much on
their very famous claim to fame. My expectation had been to find a myr-
iad of Doc Holliday burger bars and Wild West saloons. However my observations had only accomplished sighting the not so wild, yet oh so
healthy, McDonalds and Kentucky establishments which had been visible
on all the street corners of my roadway so far. "Fairly peculiar," was the
phrase used, as in every other region that I had so far visited in North
America, the merest hint of a connection to any possible claim to fame is
milked to the enth degree. Steering Horris to the pavement we stopped
and asked a local fellow the whereabouts of the OK Corral. My inquiry
was met with a surreal expression of deep thought, painted across his
face. Pleasingly the thought then changed its suit into a pleasant verbal
admission of ignorance, but then offered me the information on the location of Boot hill, which was gladly received. Following the chap's directions Horris and I set forth on our way up to Boot Hill to visit the museum which was apparently also part of the same exhibition, and I made
the assumption that we would also probably find a certain Corral for
which we had been searching also in this locality. Leaving my companion
securely parked, a survey of the "old town museum" began. They had
obviously built a replica street for the tourist, which was thoughtful of
them, though surveying the area I did appear to be the only traveller who
had bothered to make the long trip across country. Preparing to be over-
whelmed by the exhibition I started at one end of the street and visited all
the different stores. They had been filled with antiques from the period,
which I have to begrudgingly admit, were rather interesting. Whether or
not it was done deliberately I shall never know, but the shops did all seem
to have the appropriate smell about them. The last building to be entered
in the street turned out to be a small museum containing the history of
Dodge and the surrounding Wild West. Also, found floating around in

period costume, was a sweet young lady with a moderately bad stutter, doing her best at being in character with the fake old town. She ushered me through the museum, with a hilarious single slap on the thigh and a loud Yee Haa, and then out through the back to finally encounter Boot Hill. Now an admission on my part is that my pre conceived image of Boot Hill does come from Hollywood. My expectations had a long dusty path leading up to a hill surrounded by a broken down old picket fence within which one would find the graves of many a lost soul. My imagination was more than three flying miles from what I actually found. Walking out from the rear of the building I entered what seemed like a small yard that was surrounded by a tall fence through which you were not able to see. Though to help the period feeling you could just behold a few modern road signs showing their faces over the top of the structure, which of course helped create an authentic atmosphere!

The five modest steps that it took for me to reach the sparse display of gravestones left me with a pail overflowing with disappointment. Once again they all wore a coat of cheap tatty falsehood having been badly "aged " by whoever had designed the whole fake town. Turning my head to read a sign in the cemetery I was at least able to knead a small amount of interest out of my disappointed frame as it did turn out that it was once actually part of the original Boot Hill graveyard, though all the bodies had long since been moved away. Retracing my sparse amount of steps I strolled back into the fake, old town building. My disappointment was balanced with the knowledge that the OK Corral obviously could not be in such an unworthy locale, so making an audacious guess I believed the city elders must have invested their money on making a really fabulous display of their most famous piece of heritage somewhere else in town. The sweet young girl in the Calamity Jane dress was once again found and asked the important question of the whereabouts of the famous Corral that I had come all the way to see. She gave me a scandalously blank look, and then advised me she had absolutely no idea where it was located, only that it definitely wasn't in Dodge! Oh dear, a small navigational error would appear to have occurred, I had been sure the Corral was in Dodge, so I had just made a four hundred mile detour to see a pretty poor fake old town, oh well never mind. Bidding farewell to Miss Calamity she gave one last thigh slap and Yee Ha, as though having to make up a certain quota per day.

Finding Horris I saddled him up and trotted out of town heading into the sunset in true western fashion, and with a perusal of the map we broke into a gallop spraying dust from our tyres and headed for our next port of call which was going to be Amarillo in Texas. Motoring onwards we followed the route 56 until crossing back into Oklahoma, and here we found a large service station in which we made a home for the night. Having arranged the interior of Horris for my regulation sleeping position, I took myself inside the large truckers restaurant to treat myself to a big slap up meal to help overcome the disappointments of the day. Ordering a ten-ounce burger meal I was delivered what seemed like at the time almost a whole cow between two pieces of bread. How I was supposed to be able to eat all of this I didn't know, but feeling that it would have been most rude to complain, I graciously tucked in and munched my way through to the point of my stomach well nigh breaking my ribs!

The day had been with hindsight, actually rather funny. We had made an enormous detour to see an extremely famous location and quite typically of me had managed to travel a goodly mileage to visit the wrong place! When squeezing my great fat burger filled belly back into Horris I noticed that we had covered a total of 338 miles during the day.

CHAPTER

EIGHTEEN

Cadillac's Have Big Bulls!

During my night's slumbers I found myself to be relatively chilly, although it was nothing compared to what had already been experienced on the excursion so far, but all in all I slept tolerably well.

The main expectation of the morning was to progress through the day without making any humongous navigational errors while on the way to Amarillo. I believed it wouldn't be too hard to achieve as it is quite a straightforward route and also whatever was going to happen, I'm sure would pale into insignificance compared to my previous day's slight diversion. To engage a splendid kick-start to the day, I went back into the service station and ordered a huge pot of their lovely "truckers" coffee, the caffeine no doubt doing me no end of harm, but at least it did fire up my metabolism into a happily wide-awake state. Another substance, which is supposedly bad for your person that I have managed to succumb to on this journey, is sugar. A goodly age was spent slowly weaning myself from the sweetness in my coffee, and I moaned bitterly about how foul it tasted without the spoonful of sweet granules that I always added. Once upon the roadway with Horris, and after visiting my first truckers restaurant my abstention was thrown quickly out of the window, due in no small part to the proliferation of free coffee that always comes with your food and the abundance of tempting sugar which is always placed on the table. The mind within reconciled the guilt with the fact that I needed the extra energy the sugar would give to keep me alert on the Interstate upon which I was traversing. Besides, I was on a tight financial budget for the whole excursion, so anything that was going to be given away for free I felt morally responsible to myself to eat!

Riding the long grey strip of tarmac once again it didn't take us too long to cross over the border into Texas within the vicinity of the town of Stratford. At that moment feelings arose of another important milestone having been completed in my tour of the States, as when leaving the lustrous buildings of Toronto I couldn't even begin to imagine the line on the map reaching this far. As my mind turned over it realised there couldn't have been too many Englishmen that have motored through Texas in a Morris Minor, which has to be said, gave me a rather splendid feeling within.

When the wheels stopped turning in Amarillo, according to my wristwatch it was about eleven thirty, then it was to the feet for ten minutes for a healthy stroll about while trying to encounter a phone box. Thankfully a contact had been given to me to telephone in the shape of Dave who was the boyfriend of an friend of mine from Toronto. He had previously rather kindly offered me a bed for the night if I happened to end up making it to Texas and Amarillo. Of course, this wasn't an opportunity to be missed as the thought of a soft mattress to stretch out on by now had attained an exceedingly large appeal.

I phoned Dave and received some directions to the location his house, then proceeded to spend a good half an hour getting lost again in the town while trying to follow my course. Needless to say I did eventually see the error of my ways and ultimately find his dwelling. With greetings made and more lovely Texan coffee drunk Dave and I set off in his car for lunch. The food gladly eaten we drove down to the Palo Duro Canyon that is situated a little to the south east of Amarillo.

The area of the Palo Duro is said by the natives to be the Grand Canyon of Texas, so when we drove down onto the chasm from the main roadway the stunning formations left me in complete agreement with the sentiments of the locals, as I was nothing less than in awe of the surroundings. The whole area about where we were standing was the region in which the Comanche Indians made their last stand in their desperate struggle against the US army. They, of course, were slaughtered while battling the greater firepower and number of soldiers they found fighting against them. Peace with the government finally came in 1875 but it meant that these noble people had to capitulate and go to live on designated Indian reserves, and of an original population of 30000 around 11000 descendants are alive today.

Dave and I went for a cheerful stroll up onto the sides of the canyon climbing over rocks and crevices with a youthful air about us. Here it was that I saw my first natural cactus actually growing from the ground, although it wasn't one of the tremendous ones (they're in Arizona) it was still big enough to hurt if your curiosity were to engage you in too close a contact. My initial rather naive reaction when first laying eyes upon its form, was to ponder why someone had come to the canyon and planted it there, for surely it would die. This I suppose was a fairly logical assumption to make on my part. Having never seen one before in its natural environment, the cactus did look rather strange sitting there growing in the ground, as opposed to sitting in a pot on someone's windowsill. I surmised that this was something I would have to get used to now having arrived in the hot western side of the US. On our ramble back down to the car, I engaged in the typical tourist pastime and partook in the obtainment of many photographs of this lovely area, and then jumping back into our transport we directed ourselves off to see a famous ranch. I hadn't quite grasped Dave's stratagem until we arrived at the ranch itself. My imagination had seen something with horses and cows which to be honest didn't supply me with all that much excitement, but on arrival I realised my misjudgement as this was the Cadillac ranch. The metallic display is made up of a row of 50's Cadillac's buried nose down in the ground standing in alignment to one another in the middle of a field. We obviously wanted to walk out to the vehicles to partake in a more scrupulous perusal, but unfortunately the field also contained a herd of cows and a somewhat mean looking, enormous bull. A courageous judgement was taken to advance on their position in a slow and relaxed manner, hopefully without the bull reasoning that we had any ulterior fondness for his herd, which we certainly didn't have, as I personally prefer the longer haired version! Halfway across no mans land, and the tension was palpable. We had been observed, and at that moment were being eyed by what seemed like an increasingly aggressive and jealous bull. Now was the time to take a photograph, which came about by the result of a unanimous resolution between the pair of us, and honestly, you do get a better appreciation of the Cadillac's from about fifty yards distance! Our antagonist by this time had started to move so without much deliberation a retreat was made, or should I say, a hasty retreat as it did involve some ardently gallant running back to the fence and the safety of the car parked on the other side.

Sitting with hearts still beating Dave spoke of an establishment where if you could eat your dinner within an hour you would be given it for free. Seeming like a thoughtfully generous overture we motored off to investigate. When walking through the door I began to realise that it probably wasn't going to be as easy a task as I had previously thought. Hanging proudly upon the door was a roll call naming the members of the populace who had managed this wondrous achievement, and it numbered only in the region of about fifty people. I then moved further along into the restaurant and beheld the photo gallery of these fine "athletes". Well without being what might be perceived as perhaps a trifle rude, it has to be said that they actually were merely a huge gathering of horribly obese kinsmen, who I'm sure will end up spending the later years of their lives plugged into cardiac equipment in their local hospitals.

Now the dinner, as it turned out, primarily consisted of a 72oz steak, which essentially gave the appearance of being the size of possibly half a cow. Additionally to this, you had rolls, a salad, some shrimp and you had to clear the plate to win, if you failed in this brave task it would cost you $32.00! Having already had a meal at lunchtime, which was in itself moderately large, and as my travelling budget was quite small for the tour, I determined not to attempt the challenge. I hope that my actions are not later seen as cowardly, but I felt to prevail I would doubtless have to starve for at least a week and be flush enough in the wallet department to be able to yield if necessary with a deal of grace and decorum.

Nonetheless after what was still a most fine normal size meal we got up to leave and I took the opportunity to scrutinise their hall of fame once again. All of the people in the pictures were no less than 20 stones in weight with distended bellies to match. After viewing the appalling scene, I realised that it would have been impossible to fit this colossal amount of food into my 10 ½ stone frame, so I gave myself a mental pat on the back for resisting the temptation.

Upon our return to Dave's house I told the story of my trifling detour to visit the sight of the Gunfight at the OK Corral, and how I was somewhat disappointed to find that I had gone all the way to Dodge City only to find that it was the completely wrong place. Anecdote told, I expected everyone to jump up and immediately tell me where the real location actually was. Unfortunately no jumping occurred within my sight at all. When I then implored if anyone did know where the corral was I was met with a wave of varying answers, all pointing me to different regions in the state of Texas. A pile of history books were then referred to, for I expressed the opinion that I didn't particularly feel the compulsion to go on any more wild goose chases in my search for the Corral, and only when I had seen it in writing would I accept having found its true whereabouts. After a goodly amount of page thumbing my nemesis turned out not to even be in Texas! The OK Corral lives in Tombstone Arizona! With the great debate of the evening finally concluded with a positive outcome I lay my exhausted head down on the splendid pillow and my fat food filled belly down on the equally splendid bed for another wonderful night's sleep, we had managed to cover 171 miles during the day.

CHAPTER

NINETEEN

Cold Snow to Hot Keys

Having had a wonderfully good night of rest, I felt positively refreshed and was raring to go. Over a lovely slap up breakfast the television was turned on to review the selection that the weather had taken regarding its days activities. After much deliberation over my next objective, the conclusion was come to that heading in a southwesterly direction would be my best course of action for the day. My previous loose plan had been to head to the Northwest and on to Santa Fe to see the mountains up there, but after seeing the morning's weather forecast, which showed about a foot of snow falling on this district I decided against it and judiciously chose to head away from the impending cold. The other rather first-rate thing about the new route was that according to my map, I would be able to pay a visit to the famous (or so everyone said) Carlsbad Caverns, which was a rather uplifting thought, as you can never really beat a good cave every now and then!

I departed my friend's house leaving a whole saddlebag full of gratitude behind for their generous hospitality and then turned my machine back out onto the thin line of tarmac pointing South.

For the first few miles it was noticed that there was a small amount of snow falling from the sky, and so with fingers crossed I hoped like a mad thing that we were leaving it behind us in our wake. The instructions for Horris were to put on a bit of a spurt enabling us to escape the leading edge of the snowfall. Of course, this was because the last thing that I desired was to be caught in any form of blizzard. Ten minutes later and my concern had been realised, not unsurprisingly the weathermen had accomplished the feat of getting their forecast completely wrong. The snow was now falling extremely heavily and soon transformed itself into a full-scale tempest. With eyes wide open as I slid along, the recollection came to me how when setting out on this little excursion, I didn't even think that it snowed in Texas. How wrong my thoughts had proven to be!

The grey matter's forward thinking had chosen once again take the back roads for my day's route, the reasoning mainly being because there was no Interstate going directly to the objective of Carlsbad. Now traversing these backwater byways in a full scale arctic storm did prove to be quite an interesting experience. Most of the time was spent sitting there shivering in my seat praying that Horris wouldn't break down as we slipped and skidded all over the brilliant white landscape. The snow lasted for about two hundred miles of the day's motoring and unsurprisingly pleasure exuded from my pores when it finally chose to abate. Visions of being stranded in the middle of nowhere with towns at about sixty mile intervals hadn't sat comfortably upon my mind. As you never saw a soul between the communities, and then hardly anyone once in the townships themselves, breaking down was not a thought I chose to dwell on for too long!

Entering into the state of New Mexico the snow was still lightly falling but thankfully with a greatly calmed fury when I stopped in the town of Roswell for a refill of both body and car. Roswell was made famous as the place where an alien spaceship was supposed to have crashed in the 50's. Being aware of this fact had me looking deeply into the eyes of some of the locals, but unfortunately no alien influences could be detected, which was rather disappointing.

It is safe to say that we did manage to eventually fight our way through the storms and arrive in Carlsbad at roughly two thirty in the afternoon. Having stopped and asked a local fellow for the whereabouts of the caverns I was directed a further twenty miles outside of town to a place called White City which was situated almost on the edge of the Guadalupe mountains. From here, you overtax your motor up a lonely mountain path to expectantly find the entrance to the cave. By the time of my arrival, it was, it has to be said, quite chilly in the extreme and purely to add insult to injury was blowing a howling gale as well. I suppose my expectations should have been more gracious to the prevailing conditions and not quite so surprised. After all I was standing on top of a mountain in December! Handing over my money at the entrance the guide took a group of us down into the caverns, it remains a constant fifty-six degrees inside the passageways so thankfully the shivering stopped and the awe-inspired enjoyment began. The range of caverns that we were being taken into are apparently the largest in the world above sea level and were formed millions of years ago when the area about was covered by the sea. The passageways of the mountains extend out in all directions, to this date around twenty-eight miles have been explored, but there are endless regions that still await the torchlight of the intrepid underground adventurer.

Our tour took around two hours to complete and was found to be a most engaging experience indeed. The magnitude of some of the subterranean "rooms" that we passed through were quite breathtaking in their enormity. The stunning formations of the many stalagmites, stalactites and other rocky type formations were, it has to be said without a shadow of a doubt, far and away the best that I have ever had the good fortune of laying my eyes upon. For the hike down into the caves we were made to follow a convoluted pathway which wound its way down and down into the first expanse of a cavern. At the end of the tour when it was time for the return journey, we were able to take a lift back to the surface, which was rather civilised. Though in fact even if you had felt in a wonderfully healthy frame of mind, and had desired to make the walk back out on your own two feet, for some reason this was strictly forbidden and thus using the lift was compulsory.

Stepping back outside into the cold was to a fair extent quite a shock for my system. The wind was by now blowing a howling gale with a somewhat finger and nose numbing wind chill being carried along for good measure. Horris who was sitting forlornly where I had left him in the carpark was the target as my frozen frame sprinted across to his sanctuary. If a car could look benumbed my poor Morris was clothed in the expression from the moment my eyes first laid upon him. Jumping in and starting him up did thankfully at least get a little heat flowing around us from somewhere. We pointed our icy noses back down the mountain road from where we had previously ascended, and motored back into White City. Now according to my guide there was supposed to be a Youth Hostel somewhere in the locality. I had a look around but on my first scouting mission failed miserably in my objective. Choosing to ask in the local garage while filling up with some more fuel, a YHA sign pinned to the wall was noticed. Apparently the owners of the garage ran the hostel, which is made up of an arrangement of rather Mexican looking stone single storey chalets. I wasn't at all surprised that my evening's shelter had been missed having already driven past them about three or four times, as they appeared unlike my expectation of what a Hostel would normally look like. The feeling overcame me that these were actually used as motel rooms for most of the time, only becoming a Youth Hostel when the combination of empty beds and hungry youths made an appearance at the same time!

I had procured some boxed Lasagne from the Garage while picking up my keys for the room. This was, as I explained to them, under the strict agreement that they would heat it up for me in the garage microwave. The owners came forth with a goodly heap of protestations claiming how heating food was very much against the regulations of the establishment, but having illustrated to them, literally on a piece of paper the economics of the situation they finally gave in and I had myself a nice hot meal. By the time my roasting hot lasagna had been polished off, and my frame had wallowed in a nice sizzling bath my stomach was starting to feel perhaps a little peckish again. As there was no way that I was going to venture outside in the cold once more on this day, an alternative source of hot or at the very least, warm nourishment had to be found.

Scanning the room I noted that the heating system consisted of a grill in the wall that contained three wire coil-heating elements, which were already blasting away at full power in an attempt to warm my quarters for the night. The realisation immediately hit me that with the heat disgorging from the wall I did indeed have something to cook on, or rather against, for another meal! Now as for foodstuffs for my diminutive feast, the travelling larder consisted of the tremendous ingredients that follow, three quarters of a loaf of bread, one apple and a bottle of orange juice, not the greatest choice in the world for my supper, but I knew it would do. The choice was made to go with the chef's evening special of hot apple surprise on toast, the surprise part was whether or not it would end up being edible! The apple was balanced on the top of the grill religiously being turned at the strike of every minute; as for the toast it caused a little bit more of a problem. Attaching the slices to the front of the grill enabling me to brown at least four slices at a time was causing something of a problem. Gravity was making his presence unwelcomely felt and pulled at least one slice to its doom on the floor, which left me with the feeling of somebody not playing a fair game of cricket. Scratching my head for a while in deep thought the pressure piled on to find a solution to the supper on the floor problem. I didn't have long to think up a crafty plan, as by now the apple was well on its way to a condition of being fully cooked. Then as if by magic a brain wave flooded my vacant lot. Grabbing the Morris keys I carefully pulled four of them from the keyring, gave the ageing fellows a quick clean, skewered each piece of bread, and hung the four slices from the grill! The combined smell of cooking apple and toast transformed me into a high state of splendidness, which I was most pleased with as by now the temperature both outside and inside had really started to drop. It was strange how the cold seemed to be pervading into the room straight through the solid stone walls, and I was extremely surprised that they appeared to be giving no form of insulation. With my peculiar meal cooked and gladly consumed I removed my finger and thumb from the cup of water to examine the carefully made key shaped burns that I had managed to strangely acquire. My body replete with lovely 'a la carte' key nourishment, I took to the bedstead while leaving the heater on at full power. Even with these actions I still had to go to bed with all my clothes on as by now it had reached a positively freezing state within the room. The rather cold and unexpectedly snowy day had surprisingly managed to produce a rather pleasing 298 miles from Horris and myself.

CHAPTER

TWENTY

Gregarious Mexicans

Rising with freezing breath at an early hour, I had the hope in my mind that we could get on the road and with a modicum of luck make it to Arizona by the end of the day. It was a pleasant surprise upon opening the curtains to see clear snow free sky all above and around me, even though there was still a goodly chill in the air. I didn't mind too much just as long as there wasn't going to be another blizzard to fight our way through.

Upon reflection it must be admitted that I did seem to be continuously getting the hours of the day mixed up as I had already crossed two time zones by this point on the tour. On each occasion the new latitude had put the clock back by an hour, which does cause a degree of confusion to a travelling Morris driver. Thankfully no major catastrophes had so far arisen due to losing these hours, other than the afore mentioned confusion, though this is probably due more to luck, than my own judgement.

Now my road led me back down the I-180 from White City, whereupon Horris and I almost immediately re-entered the state of Texas, and from here the road wound its way up into the Cornudas Mountains. The Cornudas range differed greatly from the Appalachian and Smoky mountains that we had previously traversed, in so much as that they appeared to be virtually devoid of any vegetation whatsoever. They could almost be termed as Desert Mountains to an untrained eye.

The wind had by now really started to pick up, blowing strongly in our faces, which wasn't helping our speed at all. As is often the case when riding a bicycle, it always seemed to be a headwind that we were motoring into. Horris dishearteningly did appear to be down on power once again which was a trifle worrying. We were starting to struggle on some of the lesser-sized inclinations, which on a good day we should have been flying up with a good deal of pace. Using a small amount of brain energy, relief was found when the penny dropped on the lack of power front, upon the appearance of a sign by the roadside. The numerals claimed we were at 5800ft elevation above sea level on a distinct plateau atop the mountain range. The lack of air pressure significantly reduced Horris's horsepower, and thus also his desire to climb the precipitous roadways. When we had traversed the mountainous region we came out on to a vast barren desert. The land wasn't a sand dune filled wilderness as you would find in Africa, but one made of hard baked dusty ground stretching out as far as the eye could see. The road speared off onto the horizon carrying a ruler straight line with it as it went. Some earnestly relaxed driving would be called for during the rest of the day.

Following the line for a few hours to where the earth meets the sky, we rolled into the city of El Paso that sits astride the Rio Grande River and forms the border town with Mexico. Hunting around for a good location to leave Horris was proving to be somewhat difficult until happily stumbling across the civic centre. Here was a parking area with the required empty spaces, one of which we commandeered and declared as a little piece of England for the afternoon. There didn't seem to be anyone around who wanted paying due probably to all the cars having permits upon their screens, so I fated to leave Horris to his own devices and crossed my fingers in the hope that he wouldn't be towed away. Finding myself now on foot, they carried me at a goodly stride down towards the border post to make an attempt at crossing into Mexico. The town I noted while walking through, is fairly small but obviously has a somewhat Mexican flavour about it and the closer you get to the border, the more the architecture leaves behind the straight concrete buildings of the US and begins to carry a much more European feel within itself. I arrived at the border post at what appeared to be the same time as everyone else who had ever intended on making a crossing. Thankfully though, as my feet were carrying me over it didn't take too long to be allowed through. It would have been fun to have brought Horris over and to have had a drive in Mexico for the day, but unfortunately my already extortionate insurance didn't cover me for driving anywhere other than Canada and the US. When looking into the cost of a days cover in Mexico I realised it would have severely broken my already tight budget. Besides, having seen the great long queue of cars on either side of the border that didn't appear to be moving at all, it obviously would have been necessary to spend most of the day sitting in a traffic jam whilst crossing in both directions.

The town of Ciudad Juarez, situated in the state of Chihuahua, sits directly opposite El Paso on the Mexican side of the frontier and strolling down the dusty hill from the barrier between the two countries, you can immediately feel and see the difference. The buildings are all low storey with an unkempt demeanour about them. Hanging from anything that could have something hung off it, were hundreds of tourist bargains, sombreros, straw donkeys, trinkets, and little Spanish toy guitars. Sauntering down the main street the shop keepers were most definitely into the hard sell, almost pleading with you on their children's lives to enter into their shops.

The first time when approached, I in a gullible fashion followed my freshly acquired best friend inside and was given the full tour of the shop, starting with the tiny Mexican jumping beans, then all the way up to a life size straw donkey. I was genuinely interested in all of the goods that they proffered me though due to a lack of space and cash, had no intention of buying any for my journey home. My nice friend even produced a can of coke for me to drink, which was most pleasant, as it had surprisingly become quite warm. Having finished the tour I thanked my host profusely for his time and bade him farewell. While passing out of the door he called out something in Spanish to me, which unfortunately wasn't quite understood, though my assumption was, that it was a parting shopkeeper pleasantry! Carrying on my promenade down the high street popping in and out of the many shops, I realised the reason why the patrons were so eager to cajole you into their own establishments by the time I passed through the third set of doors. It was simply because they all were selling essentially the same tourist goods merely rearranged in a different manner within all the differing showrooms. While standing outside one of the establishments, a fellow struck up a conversation with me regarding the lack of variety and quality of the products that were on offer in the town. He also commented how sad it was that people who were only visiting his country for a day like myself, should never see what he described as the real Mexico. Agreeing with him on this point I explained that I thought it better to at least see this small part rather than none at all. Nodding his head, my latest acquaintance then suddenly had an amazing piece of inspiration, what he could do, purely for me of course, would be to take me on a special tour of all the local markets that the day-trippers never normally see, and as luck would have it his car was parked right there in front of us by the kerbside! This fellow's generosity I found to be quite overwhelming. How fortunate it was that he happened to be parked by the side of the road on the main street of town when I happened along. Friendliness to this degree by fellow man was felt to be wholly warming. It was with considerable sadness that I had to turn down his thoughtfully kind offer as by now I didn't actually have too much time left to go off exploring the towns markets. Upon entering the last shop on the high street some money found its way out of my wallet as the owner probably had the least amount of trade due to his poor location. A large traditional poncho made of real wool was acquired which will be a splendid memento of my days sojourn in Mexico. Walking back towards the border I came across my friend with the car again making the same altruistic offer that he had made to me to another tourist. This fellow's cup of generosity was surely overflowing, so a mental note was made that I must visit Mexico again one day to meet more of these lovely people.

Having navigated the way through the frontier once again and returned to El Paso in the US, a quick paced amble back up through the town was taken. Turning down a side road I happened across an army surplus store, which was jam-packed to the brim with clothes, gadgets and other various ex army paraphernalia. Wandering around it was like an Aladdin's cave of differing objects, assuming of course that Aladdin had the intent to wage his own small war somewhere. I chose to ignore all the guns and knives as these, especially the guns, are designed for only one purpose and that is to kill. The love affair that is held in this country between men and their armaments is all wrapped up and passed down from the history of the Wild West, and the universal weapon carrying society of that time. What they don't seem to have quite grasped yet, is that in modern society the likelihood of being in a gunfight in a saloon is to some extent unlikely to happen. If these people really do want to own a gun they should also be forced to give up their cars for a horse and live the true cowboy's lifestyle out on the prairie. I'm sure this would prove that the ownership of a gun was purely to have an item used to bolster their own personal machismo. Even though the clothes in the store were of obviously good quality, I didn't actually need anything else to wear, so ended up happily finding and purchasing a set of superbly thick leather gloves of the type that I had been seeking for months.

Retrieving Horris from where he had been left, I am happy to recount that he had remained thankfully unmolested by parking attendants, and so my joy encouraged me to make a quick oil and water check to make sure everything was topped up as it should be. Motoring away from El Paso on the I-10 we crossed the Rio Grande River and a pretty unimpressive flow it was too, but I had crossed it now all the same. Our route also then had us passing over the Continental Divide. An admission on my part is that I only knew of the great moment because there was a large sign that boldly proclaimed the fact to the passing motorist. Many things seem to come in threes, and my third of the afternoon was to be the San Andreas

Fault. The crack in the earth's crust starts in Southern California and heads unerringly northwards for 600 miles before turning out into the Pacific Ocean. Many earthquakes occur along the unsteady edges of the two great plates, I had hoped to experience one of these first hand but with regret all was quiet during the time of my visit. The mountains about me were now ascending in gigantic barren sylvan peaks, and perhaps due to having ingested too much of the mountainous cold air, when reaching the town of Deming I had dishearteningly started to feel somewhat under the weather. Pulling off the roadway for an interlude found me marching over to enter an elegant Mexican restaurant, for the sole purpose of filling myself with Nachos and coffee as a therapeutic measure. The food was most delicious and certainly filled an empty gap that had formed within me, but unfortunately didn't help too much with the cold like symptoms that were by then descending about my person. I purchased some aspirin in a local Drug store in a further attempt to elevate the pervading grottyness that was gradually overtaking my body, but by this time it was too late as I had now got a full blown cold or even possibly the dreaded flu. Oh dear! Crossing over several more mountains, about which I was now becoming perhaps a little blasé, we pulled off the road into a nice rest area situated just inside the border of Arizona. Using a goodly amount of thought, the realisation then came upon me that having any sort of illness on this excursion, be it a sniffle of a cold or the horrendous flu, is thoroughly silly, superfluous to my requirements, and is in reality, quite unnecessary. With my mind made up I then resolved that all further symptoms of these aggravations would have to have departed my frame by the next morning! At the time of my eyelids closing for the day we had covered 309 miles.

CHAPTER

TWENTY ONE

Bribes, Guns and Grenades

It was in the company of happiness that I was able to report that the new sleeping bag that Dave allowed me to borrow on the previous day in Amarillo was a great deal warmer than the paper thin version that I had been laying my weary head within to this point of the journey. From this I am sure that you can deduce that I at least had a warm nights sleep. Lamentably the flu and its accompanying aches and pains, against my strict instructions, had chosen to remain with me until the morning. Therefore due to the germs, I managed to complete only a restless few hour's slumber, which was felt to be rather an inconvenience to a travelling Morris driver. Once I had extricated myself from my new sleeping quarters we were soon back on the tarmac and the constitution did feel perhaps marginally better due probably to the familiar movement of Horris. Pleasure engulfed me as Horris pulled off the road into the first truckers stop. This was for the sole purpose of getting my morning fill of the special strong revitalising coffee that they serve only in this type of establishment. Gulping down a number of cups the almost neat caffeine had my eyes wide open and my body all charged up. Before it had a chance to wear off I rushed outside and gave Horris a service. The maintenance included as a special gratuity the fitting of some new spark plugs, and even the gift of a new sump full of oil. My enthusiasm and probably caffeine ran out when the thought went through my mind to also change the gearbox and back axle oil on my friend as an extra special treat for his fine accomplishments. Rather than grovelling about on the floor changing some more oil, I amazingly found myself back inside drinking my way through another pot of coffee, it had been a tough fought election but not that unsurprisingly, the coffee had won over the gearbox with a landslide victory.

We pulled back out onto the I-10 and Horris was pointed in the direction of Tombstone. I was seriously hoping that this time, with a little good fortune, we would actually find the location of the OK Corral, the real Boot Hill, and forgo any more "wrong town" experiences like the ones in Dodge City and accomplish the task without having to use the words wild, goose, and chase!

We trundled into the town of Tombstone which a wayfarer had unequivocally assured me was the location that I desired and as luck would have it, (and I'm sure it was all down to luck and not good navigation), it did indeed turn out to be the legitimate location of the gunfight for which I was searching. Quite remarkably all the original buildings were still standing which was rather nice to see after my disappointment in Dodge. My initial duty, now that it been confirmed that we had arrived in the correct town, was of course to take a photograph of Horris in front of the famous OK Corral. It was here in 1881 that the Earp brothers fought a daring gun battle with the Clanton gang outside the Corral. Now over a hundred years later, a Morris Minor stood ready to tread upon the same ground. My picture appeared to be quite an easy exercise, as all I would have to do was to stop on the fairly quiet street, jump out and take Horris's likeness. Of course in reality, the process turned out to be somewhat more complicated, which to be honest, is thankfully the normal way that things generally happen for me. With a distinct position spied out, I drove around the block and came back down the street ready to pull into the pavement for the shot in front of the Corral. At the very moment I was about to complete the manoeuvre, a huge silver Greyhound coach reversed into my spot completely blocking the view of the required Corral! This was found to be somewhat of a nuisance and even more so when the coach started to disgorge what appeared to be numerous amounts of corpulent photo taking tourists. They of course, all hung around the very place that I didn't want them to be and also, to make matters worse, carried a rather lugubrious demeanour about themselves. Even if the coach hadn't been there, their herd like presence would have probably swept us up and carried us off if I hadn't been fortunately encased in a Morris!

While they all stood nearby clicking away with their cameras, I chose in true western fashion to form a defensive circle with my wagons. Well I didn't actually have any wagons, only a Morris and as there was only one of us, making a circle proved to be a trifle awkward, so awkward in fact that most distastefully, the fleshy hoards had beaten me to it and appeared to be encircling me.

Horris and I now had our parking position in custody with handbrake firmly on and so started to plot and plan our next move. After a while the chubby ones started to move away, having probably used up all of their Nikon arrows on the advance to the Corral. Thankfully this solved the crowding problem about the locality that I had chosen to monopolise, but lamentably the huge Greyhound coach was still very much in the way. The only option that I felt was left open to me was to ram the coach out of the way, so revving up Horris engine the clutch was dropped, we flew across the road in clouds of tyre spinning smoke and made a huge impact on the rear! No, No, hang on a minute another hair raising Wild West location has got the better of me again! In truth I hoofed it across to the coach, not in any smoke, and knocked on the drivers window with the extremely polite request for him to move his vehicle. The negotiations were to some extent tough and drawn out, but in the end he did see the reason in my argument, or to put it another way the colour of the $10 it cost me to induce him to move. It is the most capitalist country in the world I suppose, so using green backs to help you win arguments is probably quite a common occurrence! There now appeared a nice big clear space to park in for the photo session, so I manoeuvred Horris about just like a professional photographer until completely satisfied with the angles, light and all those important photograph type things! I turned round after making the final adjustment to the arrangement of Horris, stood on my mark and was almost about to take the picture when a large white and blue pick up truck pulled up right in the middle of the picture! "No, no" I bemoaned, "You cannot park there". The good old boy who was driving the truck gave me a variety of a drawling, obscene Southern response, the essence of which when translated simply meant "sorry old chap I'm not moving". The tone of his voice and look on his face I believe has been lost in the translation to text! So my excellent photo ended up with Horris, the OK Corral and also a large white and blue truck in the frame, I suppose it gives the picture a balance between the old and the new wild west though I don't feel completely convinced.

The OK Corral

While walking away to have a look around the town, I pondered to myself what Wyatt Earp and his gun-slinging friends would have thought if they could see the scene before the Corral today. It certainly is distinctly different to the view that they were all used to in their time. Having wandered around the shops and scrutinised the entire gun slinging memorabilia, Horris was retrieved and we moseyed on out of town into the sunset and found our way to Boot hill. On our arrival I was most pleased to discover that it was the original graveyard and not another tourist fake as in Dodge. They had a huge gravestone at the entrance, in front of which I placed my friend for his obligatory photograph, all of which occurred without the slightest drama or adventure, which did feel most unusually strange. Leaving Horris in the official parking place, I went for a stroll amongst the graves. As in all war cemeteries around the world, the ages on the gravestones were of young people killed in the prime of their lives. I would imagine a good deal of them had chosen the life of the gunslinger at an early age and paid the ultimate price to the hand of a more experienced shot.

The difference I noticed between Boot Hill and a military cemetery though, was that in the latter, the victims of such youthful waste are always given a deal of respect and dignity in their final resting place, whereas here in Boot Hill, they were all laid out in a disorganised manner as though no one especially cared. Mulling over the burials, I supposed that at the end of the day in both cases young lives had been lost to other men's bullets, and when they fell to the ground, I'm sure they were none too concerned about the arrangement of the graveyard in which they were to finally rest. A couple of the gravestones stood out and are worth repeating here.

John Heath taken
from county jail and
lynched by Bisbee mob
in Tombstone Feb 22 1884

Here lies Lester Moore,
four slugs from a 44,
no less,
no more.

It was now time to blow on out of Tombstone, and away we flew with tumbleweeds at our sides to start on the road to the Grand Canyon. As we passed Tucson the famous western style cactus started to emerge within the scenery. The further the miles rolled beneath our wheels, the more numerous amounts of these strange plants started to appear scattered about the area as far as the eye could see. We were unmistakably now in the real Wild West!

Once more the mountains were now getting rather on the large side and they vexatiously did again cause us a few problems on the slow climbs to the summits. Thankfully by now, previous experience had shown that a general slow plodding would eventually get us to the top, so the knowledge of the method was called on again at this time, and on further numerous occasions throughout the day.

Several miles before reaching Phoenix I pulled off the interstate following a seedy old broken-down sign that had a tremendous arrow pointing to the next exit saying "Gas". I duly followed the rudimentary instructions that took me right off the main road and off into the local hills. When reaching the point of retracing my steps, lo and behold a run down disaster of a garage that sported only two pumps appeared on the horizon. I pulled on to their unkempt earthen forecourt not really knowing if the place was even still in use or not, when out of the depths of what can only be described as a shack, came Billy Bob and his associate Bobby Ray. My immediate familiarity with the names arose because American garage attendants and mechanics apparently all need to have their monogram embroidered onto the front of their overalls as some sort of national tradition. These fellows were your archetypal hillbillies, chewing tobacco masticating about behind the blackened teeth, which was then proficiently ejected through the air in a disgusting jet, coming to rest appallingly close to the position of my feet. If this was the traditional local welcome it has to be said I was just a little perturbed by the formalities. Looking beyond Billy Bob's greasy peaked baseball cap, which sat on his head for some strange reason at forty-five degrees, I noticed a desert buggy parked alongside the shack. Astonishment forced me into having a double take which involved a closer peering examination, though it was managed without venturing too far from the relative sanctuary of Horris. The Buggy was completely covered in guns, rifles, knives and almost all the other weapons that your self-respecting mercenary or general lunatic would probably be carrying. At the moment when my eyes fell upon some grenades hanging from one side of the machine, I realised that I was being watched while glaring in loathing at their Buggy. At this untimely juncture Billy Bob mouthed to me "Aint she summit". My rather deceitful yet sarcastic reply was then returned across the foul enclosure "Yes, a rather splendid instrument of death". The full truth, in certain situations, was probably better withheld from an ear that would be easily offended by it, especially if the ear was armed with enough weapons to start a small war and would have little hesitation in polishing off an old Morris and its driver. After these few tricky moments it started to dawn on Billy Bob that I would probably like to become a patron of some of the fuel that they owned, so he threw the question across to me of "Want gas?" I came back at him with a very British "Yes please" and pulled the nozzle out of the pump. "Aint none in there boy" was drawled at me as he turned and walked over to a beaten up old Jerry can that was sitting in the dirt by the corner of his hovel. Bringing it back across the yard he opened Horris fuel cap and started pouring it in losing a good deal of it onto the ground as he didn't have any form of funnel to use. When he had finished soaking the back of the car in the explosive liquid, he then asked for an extortionate amount of money for the little fuel that had found its way to the tank, probably double the actual real value. My jaw up to this point was still firmly resting on the floor with disbelief and as I was still clutching the fuel nozzle from the pump, I carefully replaced it back into the machine that obviously hadn't worked for an exceptionally long time. Call me a craven fellow, my person will accept the decoration, but I paid him the money and left, thankful that I hadn't seen any of the artillery bolted on to the Buggy used for its proper purpose. I'm sure in reality I could have misread the whole situation, probably these kind people gave me the last of their fuel, and all the guns and knives were to protect them from all of the big snakes and spiders that live out here in the wild west. If this was the case, then I humbly apologise, though personally I'm not so sure!

Leaving my hillbilly friends behind in a cloud of desert dust, we once again headed back out onto the relative safety of the main road and after a few miles came into the city of Phoenix. My stop in the town was rather fleeting and entailed giving myself the barest of "whistle stop tours". This was probably due entirely to the fact that I was so looking forward to seeing the Grand Canyon the following day that poor old Phoenix did somewhat pale in the Canyon's great shadow. With the roadway rushing beneath us we pushed on North out of Phoenix and I managed to get within about fifty miles of Flagstaff. Here tiredness caught up with me and started knocking upon my door. Withdrawing from our wanderings of the day, Horris and I pulled into a lay-by where I was gratified to be able to stop for a rest. Here sitting in the relative quiet of Horris, my imagination carried me to the following day where I hoped the splendid occasion of my long awaited view off the edge of the Grand Canyon would occur. As my eyes closed they noted we had managed to achieve a grand distance of 363 sometimes rather peculiar, miles.

CHAPTER

TWENTY TWO

Don't Fall In!

I awoke in the morning into the light of day after a rather restless nights sleep with my sniffly cold having turned overnight into the full blown flu, which has to be said was somewhat annoying, as it did tend to make one feel moderately under the weather. Thankfully after only a few miles I did manage to find a local drug store near to where my slumbers had been spent and purchased some super powerful "get rid of your cold quick" medicine which will hopefully do the trick.

After taking the foul potion, my inner soul concluded that I really should stop and have a huge breakfast to help re-energize my poor ill body, so pulling into the first suitable looking truckers restaurant, I entered and sat down. Here I hammed it up a little to the nice waitresses, and was mothered and smothered with as much food and coffee that a flu ridden Morris driver could ever possibly ingest while seated at a table.

The edibles and the very friendly people in the restaurant did go down profoundly well and once finished, I dragged my by now bloated, food filled body, outside to give Horris another good service. It's funny really, but when having eaten like a pig, I do feel duty bound to then go and work on Horris a little while so that he doesn't feel left out. Strange how the mind works! After a deal of adjustment to hopefully cure any of Horris's ills, I noticed that the engine had started to run a little rough again. This had been coming on gradually over the last few days and I just hoped that it wasn't the start of any more valve problems as before.

We set off to conquer the road again but soon stopped in Flagstaff to replenish our fuel levels. Although Horris was carrying a spare can with enough petrol in to get me to hopefully the next station, I tended to try and keep the small Morris fuel tank as full as possible. The thought of running out on one of the long stretches of deserts or mountains that we had been crossing between the towns and cities was something I had been trying to aspire towards avoiding.

During the day so far, the highest elevation that we crossed was a huge 7000 feet, so with this in mind it was assumed that it was the cause of the rough running which Horris had been displaying.

As we approached within a few miles of the Grand Canyon the landscape about us turned into arid scrubland. The great plateau was strewn with a covering of small bushes and spindly little trees on an earth that was growing no grass. The scenery about was definitely not what I had expected, but as we came up within a few hundred yards of the canyon's edge, lush vegetation started to appear, almost as though it had been placed there to hide the view from prying eyes. Imagine the early settlers who, crossing the vast expanses of desert, would see the greenery of the trees off in the distance believing them to be some sort of oasis, then on their arrival discovering the view out over to the other side for the first time. I wonder if the awesome sight that was before them brought on depression, knowing that they would have to go round to get across, or delight at the natural beauty the like of which they probably had never seen before.

It was now about 12.30 in the afternoon and my first priority was to find the Youth Hostel. This was easily accomplished as it was well sign posted, though it was still too early in the day for it to be open, so parking Horris up in a nice position my expectations carried me off towards the edge of the Canyon. Passing through the tall trees, which are all along this area, I suddenly broke through and there, laid before me in all its incredible magnificence, was the Grand Canyon. A width of 18 miles, a length of 277 miles and a depth of 5000 feet are all impressive textbook figures for a knowledgeable scholar to repeat, but are dry and boring when read from the page. Standing on the edge of the vista my eyes had never laid themselves upon something of such wonderful natural beauty. The colours, the texture, and the pure scale of the scene took the breath away almost to the point when you thought it might never be returned. I was standing on the south ridge and walked following the undulating path for about two miles. All along the trail there were no fences to stop you falling over the edge into the fabulous abyss below. The panorama was found to be truly wondrous. During my whole time there on the cliff top, I was transfixed by the view out across the vast expanse and felt an incredible pulling effect on my inner being to proceed that bit closer to the edge.

Arriving at a man-made observation point I strolled inside, but soon rapidly came out again. Here my senses found themselves observing the Canyon through sanitary plates of glass with piped music and tourist information roaring out through speakers hanging from the walls. The sterile safety of the building completely missed the whole point of being at this magical place for me, yet I understood its usefulness to the plastic burger tourist of America. Drifting back along the pathway towards the Hostel, I espied way down in the depths of the Canyon one of the mule trains loyally ferrying their cargo of garishly fleshy sightseers back up to the camper van park situated nearby. Travelling down the bridle path to the floor of the Canyon on one of the mule trains did, it must be said, rather appeal to me. Ashamedly though, the thought of the company that one might conceivably have to keep, did render the idea untenable within my mind. Any further thoughts of mule riding were lured away when on returning to the Hostel the discovery was made that the ride down for a day cost $64 and a two-day excursion was $209. My limited collection of money happily agreed that the junket was well worth the investment required, but lamentably the expense was a long way outside the budget of my journey. Now that everything was open, my gear was moved from Horris into the Hostel therefore to claim my bed for the night. Having showered and become clean to the point of being companionable, my feet carried me off down the road to procure some food and coffee to replenish my by now groaning stomach. On the way I observed some wild reindeer dashing about with gay abandon, which were soon followed by some mules. These I assumed had become tired of the backpacking life and at some stage had made their break for freedom with a good deal of success! My belly once again full with the delights of American cuisine, I headed off over to the Canyon edge to watch the sun go down. Upon reaching the edge, a nice large rock was encountered on which was placed my somewhat weary body. The brilliance of the hues that were then displayed before me as the sun started to set were quite astonishing, radiating different apparitions of colours from the surface of the rocks in an awesome display which will never be forgotten. My day was now once again over so I finished it with the final walk back to my bed in the Hostel, here happily collapsing into a lovely deep sleep having covered 121 miles during the day.

CHAPTER

TWENTY THREE

Free cake and coffee

Awaking in the morning, my senses discovered that a full-blown cold had been fated to come and stay with me awhile. This was found to be a trifle annoying as lethargy and feeling disagreeable hadn't been included on my pre-trip itinerary! Dragging the body from my sick bed before the sun had come up; I clothed myself in a scruffy manner and walked over to the Canyon edge to watch the early morning sunrise. Even though feeling moderately awful, the sights displayed before me as the sun rose over the horizon had an ethereal presence. The heavens poured sheets of enchanted colours from their cloudland easel, which verily took the breath away, the morning light picking out the textures in the rocks that during the daytime you would never see. Standing stunned at the panorama that lay before me, the realisation gradually overcame my body that the cold wind was also blowing and I was now starting to freeze. Poised gazing out over the vastness, I was starting to feel like giving in and heading back to my warm bed for the rest of the day when the eyes noticed that many of my fellow early risers had steaming cups of coffee in their hands. In the image of the Bisto kids my frozen nose followed the smell of the coffee back to the large exclusive hotel that sits on the edge of the cliffs. It was here inside the discovery was made; finely dressed waiters were giving out refreshments to the hotel guests who had chosen to enjoy the early morning views. Strolling in and standing in line in my rather dishevelled state didn't appear to cause any disturbance as I gratefully received some lovely free coffee and cake without a question being asked. My cheek did then contemplate the possibility of extending this munificence and going upstairs to find an empty room to finish off my night's sleep in the hotels five star luxury. The contemplation didn't last too long as I thought better of it and headed back outside to catch the last rays of the morning sunshine lighting up the canyon in their remarkable exhibition.

Once the sun had fully risen and the splendid display was over I took myself back to the hostel for some breakfast. Here arriving in the warm, my eyes and nose started to stream in a most convincing fashion due to the bothersome malady that was hanging over me. My sickly personage really didn't feel like facing the elements once again and doing any sight-seeing, therefore with thanks, the nice lady who was running the Hostel allowed me to stay inside for the day to help me rid myself of the annoying fever.

By the evening I was starting to feel perhaps a little bit better and so walked off to find a restaurant to fill my by now vacant lot below. On the way I beheld a six mule, mule train heading up from the Canyons edge, each animal was lashed to the one in front while they galloped back to their stables without any human company. Upon later inquires, it was discovered that it is quite a normal spectacle which had been witnessed, as the mules knew that they would be fed as soon as they returned! Both the mules and I ate well on this evening, for myself filling up with a fine chicken meal thankfully going some way to calming down my temperature. As for the mules they didn't tell me how much they enjoyed their food but I'm sure that they did.

When returning to the Hostel I bumped into some friendly people whom I had previously met in New Orleans, which was obviously a rather nice surprise. The rest of the evening was spent discussing various route plans and choosing from the westerly points of interest the most attractive place to be visited. From here I retired to my bed, having covered no Morris miles, but a fair few by foot.

CHAPTER

TWENTY FOUR

Toe Nail a Dam Picture

After partaking of the contents of the medicine cabinet I had a wonderfully deep night's sleep, happily making me feel much better than the previous few days. This outcome pleased me enormously, as it had turned out to be a fine sunny morning. After getting up and breakfasting, I set to work on Horris doing the normal maintenance and pampering jobs that he requires before we set off. With the chores completed, we turned our faces to the road for our day's drive. On the way out of town we motored into a small supermarket to replenish the stocks of travelling food and possessions like toothpaste. When walking in, much to my astonishment, there, perusing various goods was Kenny Everett and the lovely girl from his TV show, Cleo Rochos. It is my duty to tell all the males reading this scribe, that she is even more pleasing to the eye in the flesh than she seems on the television! I chose to say hello, even though I'm sure they probably really didn't want to be recognised. The reasoning behind the deed was that nobody would ever believe me upon returning home that I had actually met famous people in a supermarket next to the Grand Canyon. Bounding up to them in a silly dog like fashion, I introduced myself then had a really nice five-minute chat all about the Canyon and this part of the states. They were exceptionally friendly and very chatty and to be honest completely unlike how I had perceived their characters to be. We parted company with many good wishes all round.

Horris and I drove South heading away from the Canyon until we came to the I-40 at William's a little to the west of Flagstaff. Here the wheel of Horris was turned West, which pointed us towards the Pacific Ocean. After a while we came to the town of Seligman where it had been planned to take a slight detour on rather a famous road, this of course was the world renowned Route 66. Motoring along this macadam piece of history seemed to bring out all the hidden musical talents that to this point had been very well hidden away inside me. Spontaneous verses of all the Route 66 related and not so related songs came bursting forth in a menagerie of mongrel sounds. Unfortunately it did seem to have the effect of scaring all the local wildlife from every tree and bush while we trundled by! We were on the 66 for about fifty miles in total, and about two thirds of the way along passed through the Hualapai Indian reservation. Rejoining the I-40 at the town of Kingman we then turned almost immediately north onto the 93 heading for the Hoover dam and Boulder city. When arriving at the Hoover Dam the first impression felt was profound awe at its colossal size, though my expectations believed it to be a lot wider than it actually was. Construction of the dam was started in 1931 and was finished by the autumn of 1936, at 726 feet high and 1244 feet wide, the concrete holds back 233 square miles of water named Lake Mead. Travelling across and then parking up on the side of the road, my cognitive juices tried to devise a way of getting a good shot of Horris on the dam. I knew this was going to be rather a tricky photograph to claim for my album as the dam is the only crossing point of the Colorado River for quite some distance. Also the roadway is the main route into Las Vegas so unsurprisingly the top of the dam was full to bursting with traffic. The first attempt had me aligning Horris for the picture of the dam where I had pulled off the road. It was all to no avail though, as the whole scene regrettably wouldn't fit within the shot. I knew the only possible way was to leave him on the dam, stand a long way back and take the picture. So off we went to get into trouble. Driving down in the queue of traffic the camera was set ready for its duty. When about halfway across I pulled as far over to the right as humanly possible and stopped. In a matter of reasonably short moments all hell broke loose, horns were blaring, people were shouting and waving their arms, it even took me a while to get out of the Morris because of the closeness of the aggrieved passing traffic. When finally I was able to jump out it was straight into the long arms of the law. They had unsportingly been sneaking up on me in my blind spot from behind. As I stood there with my camera they shouted at me "NO PHOTOS" which I thought was rather discourteous, then they ordered me off the dam in no uncertain terms. By this time because of their very sloppy parking to my rear, a long line of irate traffic had built up and was throwing rather a lot of unpleasant abuse in my direction! Riding away from the dam, the first photographic failure of the journey was carefully thought about. Although we didn't get the image we had originally desired, the absurd shenanigans that had ensued in the attempt were well worth missing the photo for, even if purely to make a good story!

Motoring onwards with the dam in our mirrors we arrived at Boulder City and stopped for a refuel in a garage. With Horris topped up, and myself invigorated by the consumption of a few chocolate bars we headed out of town in the direction of Las Vegas. Before reaching there though we had to cross some more mountains, and woefully Horris was starting to acquire another rattle again. Odd noises started to emanate from even odder places and he felt quite down on power, which was causing a lot of gear usage on all the hills let alone on the mountains. Finally arriving in Las Vegas at 4 o'clock I found the Youth Hostel though regretfully it hadn't yet opened for the evening, so parking up I wended my way off to fill my belly with some trashy fast food. I knew it was a horrible substance to eat but sometimes when you get the craving there is nothing that you can possibly do! Once the inner portion of my person had been filled to an almost sickly quantity a stroll was taken back to the hostel carrying the hope of the doors now being open. Thankfully they were, therefore I paid my money, collected my key and started the search for my room. The layout of my noontide abode was quite reminiscent of a Butlins holiday camp. The design was a series of single storey chalets laid out in a large "H" pattern. Within the grounds there was an unkempt garden filling in the gaps between the legs of the "H". Pathways of subsiding and broken paving slabs guided you about, helping to finish off the overall effect. The room that I was to use for the evening was to be shared with two other fellows, both Americans, and I think quite possibly your typical small time gamblers the pair of them. Clark was thirty-five, and spent his time as an off the main strip, roulette table host. He regaled me with stories of high dollar losers and winners and how he used all of the money that he earned being a host to go and play the tables in his favourite, Caesar's Palace. He wore the most awful polyester suit with matching mauve waistcoat while the greased back hair upon his head rather helped him fit the part he seemed so keen to be playing. With Clark gone off to host his wheel, the other chalet resident put in an appearance. His name was John. He was about six foot five inches tall and for some unexplained reason was stumbling around on a pair of crutches. He reminded me immediately of Huggy Bear from Starsky and Hutch and appeared somewhat out of context in Las Vegas. John was a card player and as he admitted to me not actually a very good one, but the law of averages should swing good fortune his way at some stage he claimed, consequently he just kept on playing. John's fashion sense was certainly on a par with his co-resident of the chalet, i.e. totally awful. I felt as though I had stumbled on a throwback community from the 1970's, their dress, style of speaking and what

they were actually saying reminded me totally of all the American TV
soaps I had watched as a child. Perhaps though this was the reality behind
all the hype and neon lights of Las Vegas, maybe because no-one here
had any permanence, they were merely living out their fantasies. For the
people I was sharing a room with, this fantasy was an America of two
decades past. John seemed a good and honest fellow, but did have one
feature that made me seriously cringe all over in a rather repulsed fashion.
While sitting on my bed with a cup of coffee in hand chatting to him as
he got ready to go out for an evening of gambling, John was perched on
the bed opposite to mine which put him only about two feet away as the
crow would fly. From a carpetbag on the floor he produced a huge pair
of tailors scissors and started cutting his toenails in an unskilled and ravenous fashion. Accompanied with each cut, a small part of him would go
flying across the room with uncontrolled direction and velocity. The
thought of piles of his nails steadily building up over the months on the
inside of the chalet really did make my flesh crawl with displeasure. Not
wishing to break the inter chalet harmony I determined to simply grin,
(with lips closed) and bear what felt like a torture for the duration of his
clipping task.

Thankfully only having ten toes it didn't take too long, and after putting on his white socks and tasselled shoes I saw him out of the door and
wished him well on his evenings endeavours. He stumbled off down the
road on his crutches with the hope of once more trying to win the elusive
million at the forefront of his mind. When he was out of sight I removed
the sheets from my bed and gave them a good shake outside to reassure
myself that any remnants of Johns previous display had also departed. My
bed remade, I finished off my coffee then to my horror discovered something sitting at the bottom of the cup. The thought that I had swallowed
the drink with the added flavouring furnished by my roommate well-nigh
had me spending the remainder of the day with my head over a bucket,
but happily my inner fortitude came through and thankfully I was able to
put the gruesome thought at least little way from my mind.

When collecting some of my things from Horris I encountered a fellow called Dave from New Zealand who was standing there with a surprised look on his face admiring the car. He exclaimed that if any one had
asked him before he had come to Vegas what were the five most least
likely things he was going to see during his visit, then an Englishman driving a Morris Minor with Canadian number plates on would have certainly
made a high number on his list! After our chat we settled on heading off
up into town to check out the casinos together. Walking up the main

strip, was I found, somewhat astonishing. The dazzling neon lights made the very sky glow over the city, making you wonder at the lengths men have gone to in the quest of draining the pockets of the gullible punters trawling the streets all about us. The first main casino that we visited was named The Mirage, and to the front of the building they had constructed an immense mountain, though I do believe it was only probably made of wood and fibreglass. Whatever materials used in the construction it did give a more accurate appearance of a real fairy tale mountain than any actual peak I have ever seen. Streams and waterfalls led down from the summit and joined at the base into a great lake stretching out before the front of the building. This was impressive enough on its own but someone suggested to us to linger a few minutes longer and wait to see what happens. After a goodly amount of lingering we nearly gave up on the notion when all of a sudden in a great whoosh the whole mountain erupted and all the water coming down from the mountain and in the lake burst into fire! This was quite extraordinary, there was no smoke, purely the flames dancing about on top of the water, presumably I believed fuelled by some sort of gas released from under the surface. The spectacle under the dark evening sky was such a surprise I was almost left without words, though truly wordless I became when finding out later from a local that each time the mountain erupted, which was every fifteen minutes, it cost the Mirage casino a cool $6000! Entering the edifice, the decor lived up to the astonishing entrance with aplomb. Outlandish opulence straight from the pages of the Hollywood school of palatial design entertained every turn of the head. Amusement immediately came to the mind though, because the people who were there and spending the money were entirely out of character with the completely ostentatious interior, almost in the same way as someone who goes to a fancy dress party but doesn't bother to dress up.

I suppose this is the crux of the matter. By encouraging the people to feel that they are in a complete fantasy land, which they do with a great deal of success, they involve them in a total sense of euphoria which in turn encourages them to empty their wallets and purses of all their hard earned moneys.

Moving on through the Mirage I poured a few dollars into a slot machine in the typical tourist fashion, and admittedly didn't really bother to understand the sundry options which were used to help relieve me of my money in a somewhat speedy fashion. Watching the people play on the card tables and roulette wheels, I had to wonder how many dreams came true for people and how many hopes were dashed every day in casinos like the Mirage. It appeared that some, if not most, of the patrons had brought along all of their savings purely to try their luck on the turn of a card or the spin of a wheel. I suppose it was their own choice to make, and what encouraged them all the more was the occasional cheer going up as someone actually won the dreamed of fortune. What you never hear though are the silent steps of the destitute people leaving, having lost all that they had owned. Perhaps the city should introduce a law that makes all the casinos talk up the losers as much as the winners, I can't see it happening though.

We walked now into what I think was the central hub of the building and much to my astonishment, there in a large cage were three white Tigers. These beautiful creatures prowling up and down before the gawping crowds sickened me. I'm sure the cage size was far above the legal standard and they did have lots of rocks to climb upon, but to see three of the most majestic of animals being used as the centre piece of this money making empire left a terribly bad taste in the mouth. My fellow patrons didn't seem to grasp my point at all as I loudly spoke my feelings for anyone to hear. I merely hoped that at some point the government would put a stop to the exploitation within this building, for at least the human victims could walk out. From here we immediately left the Mirage and I thoroughly regretted having given them a few of my dollars via a slot machine. Seeing the tigers had left me frustrated and angry at the casino owners' ignorance.

We carried on afoot up the main strip calling in to all the famous casinos, Caesars Palace being the most impressive of the rest, though at the end of the day they all came down to the same thing, slot machines, roulette wheels and card tables. I'm sure we were the ideal guests managing to loose a few more dollars and spending an extortionate amount on drinks at one of the many bars that are scattered around inside of the establishment. I had heard that you get served free drinks here while gambling away your money, but I suppose this only includes the high rollers on the tables and not the humble $5.00 losers on the slot machines!

By half past two in the morning we had both run out of enthusiasm and energy so took a stroll back amid the bright lights towards the hostel. The whole city however was still well and truly alive and kicking, music playing, lights a- flashing and scores of huge American cars relentlessly cruising along the strip, motoring who knows where. Upon my arrival back at the room pleasure encompassed me when discovering that my roommates hadn't yet arrived home, thus saving the necessity of me having to shake out my bed once again, which unsurprisingly, was much to

my great relief. At the end of the day by the time my head found the pillow, Horris and I had managed to cover 275 miles.

CHAPTER

TWENTY FIVE

California Dreaming

In the morning I rose bright and early with what felt like a most splendid spring in my step. Where the energy was coming from I didn't really know. The only possible explanation that I had on the matter was the communal coffee perhaps being laced with bit of a jolly "pick me up" by my friendly roommates. They had recommended the specially ground coffee for use in the morning when leaving for their evenings gambling, so my finger of suspicion regarding the cause of my wide open eyes fell happily upon them! Skipping across the road to the Mexican restaurant for an early morning fill up of lovely Latin food, I here indulged myself in my love of Tortilla chips covered in a gorgeous meat sauce until almost fit to burst. Having eaten an evening size meal for my breakfast I did feel rather like the proverbial stuffed pig when waddling back across the road to Horris, there still obediently parked as I had left him the day before. My penance for stuffing myself to the brim was to give the car a scrupulous checking over and topping up of all the fluids that he had no doubt been gradually leaking over the previous few days. All the normal checks and adjustments that I normally do were completed in no time. The one though that I hadn't been looking forward to was now next on the list, this was topping up the gearbox oil. Of course this is quite a simple job under normal circumstances but was one that I had been avoiding meeting so far on the journey. The reason for the apprehension was entirely my own fault so I had no one but myself to blame for the oncoming struggle. You see when laying the deep pile furry carpet into Horris back in Toronto I had made sure it was rather well secured and not liable to come out again in any great hurry, the main reason for this was to improve the insulation properties of the floorpan. When coming to cut a hole in my nice carpet for the gearbox filler I resolved it was probably best left uncut to resist any chance of cold air incursion to the inside of the car. The decision had now come back to haunt me as all I now had in my possession to cut the carpet was a rather blunt keyring penknife. After what seemed like an age of sawing and stabbing away I finally broke through with blistered fingers only to find that the hole had been cut in the wrong place! With a Morris full of desperation and my body now aching from the contorted position in which I had been lying, the cut in the carpet was gradually enlarged in the rough direction of the gearbox filler hole. Finally when locating the large rubber grommet which covers the access, a large sigh of relief passed through my twisted and misshapen body!

As the moment came to top up the oil using the very expensive funnel which had been purchased in the Grand Canyon, I'm not sure if I was dismayed or overjoyed when it turned out that the gearbox didn't actually need topping up at all, though sod's law decrees that if I hadn't bothered, then of course the oil would have run out.

Upon returning to the room and collecting up my belongings, a goodbye was said to my slumbering friends, though to be honest I don't think my farewells got any way past the deep sleep they were both ensconced in.

Once again Horris and I were riding the tarmac. In this instance the particular piece of tarmac happened to be the I-15 heading for Los Angeles. After about forty-five minutes of motoring we came to a sign many people, if not most, said we would never end up seeing, and what did it say?

Welcome to CALIFORNIA!

To be honest I did actually drive straight past the sign while engaged in some slumberous driving and then it took me a good half a mile to realise the significance of the moment. Accompanied by whining gears, Horris and I reversed all the way back down along the route to claim the obligatory photo in front of the sign, which was surprisingly much to the chagrin of the on coming traffic, which I felt was most unreasonable considering the importance of the moment!

California dreaming

Standing by Horris and feeling a good degree of pride emanating from within I looked ahead to the mountains on the horizon, these were part of the somewhat grand sounding and it has to be said, also looking, East Mojave national Scenic area. I felt so pleased that we had reached this point on our little adventure as from here on, even if we broke down beyond repair, we would still have succeeded in our goal of reaching California.

We pushed on along the I-15 crossing what are known locally as the Shadow mountains, poor Horris once again putting on a brave face as he struggled to pull us up the steep inclines which seemed to constantly pan out before us. As we slowly crested the peaks and the great rush began down the long sweeping descents my enthusiasm was only tempered by the knowledge of Horris' pretty awful braking system lurking below my right foot as our only means of abating our speed in the case of an emergency. This is a knowledge though, that I had carried all of the way so far without too many problems, so with the still flowing euphoria of actually making it this far in the trip, the thought of losing the brakes wasn't at this stage going to worry me to any great degree.

Stopping in the town of Barstow to buy some fuel for both the car and my own person I entered a general store and managed to almost clear their shelves of many a bar of celebratory chocolate. I knew full well that this was bad from both a budgetary and nauseous inducing point of view, but didn't give it much real concern as I merely felt the need to devour a goodly amount of chocolate!

We were now heading for San Bernardino and much to my delight and surprise, were passed while motoring along the road, by the people that I had first met in New Orleans and had last seen only two days before in the Grand Canyon. They bellowed as they pulled along side that they were going straight on to San Francisco, and maybe they would see me there in a few days time. Their address and an invite to stay resided in my pocket so this I hoped was a real possibility.

Crossing over the last set of mountains before the long roll into Los Angeles itself, I looked before us down into the green valleys only to be shocked to see the disgusting greenish grey smog that seemed to be clinging to the hillsides like veritable poison soup. Driving down into the filthy air I could barely contemplate what horrendous things it would be doing to my lungs as I passed through its noxious clouds. We drove directly through the downtown area and managed to, of course, find ourselves in the position of being lost once again. The occurrence wasn't something that had me all that pleased, as it was one of the places that some of my dear friends had told me that I would probably get murdered in! In the end we pulled to a stop in a severely run down petrol station to appeal for directions. While locking Horris I could see all the eyes within scrutinising us in a quizzical fashion, the sight of a Morris Minor adorned with East Canadian plates was obviously a none too regular occurrence in this part of LA. Walking inside with map in hand, the occupants seemed to fit my preconceived stereotype for LA gang members down to a tee. A thought shot through my head, (rather than the bullet that I had expected) that a hasty retreat would probably be the best order of the day, but before my legs could carry me to safety one of the "gang" members asked if he could help me.

Now of course following all the rules that say, don't make yourself look like a tourist I replied, "Oh hello there, I wonder if you could help, I'm rather lost!" Now with a burst of laughter all round having already seen Horris as we pulled in and now hearing my accent they replied with a Chorus of "Dam rights you're lost buddy"! My newfound friends then studied my map (once released from my still tightly clutched hands), and kindly directed me off towards the Youth hostel in San Pedro that was located on the southern most tip of the Los Angles peninsular.

When I finally managed to happen upon my abode for the evening it had become quite dark as the twilight hours I suppose, are wont to do, and soon after parking up outside the Youth Hostels doors the breeze brought the smell of the fresh air coming off of the sea. Of course it wasn't merely any old sea, it was the Pacific Ocean, another milestone in the journey completed. By the time that I had booked in, cleaned up and had a feed for the night, we had covered another 278 morrising miles.

CHAPTER

TWENTY SIX

Goosing The Queen

At an early hour of the morning I rose to a somewhat chilly, although rather bright and sunny day, and so with a spring in my step it was determined to give Horris a bit of a check up as he had appeared to be yet again lacking in power as we had driven towards the Hostel on the previous night. My worry of course was that we might have burnt another exhaust valve, which admittedly would be rather a blow to my personal equilibrium. Opening the bonnet the familiar creaks let forth to reveal all of Horris' workings and with much listening to the exhaust pipe, compression checking, rubbing of head and scratching of chin I realised that yes, we had indeed once again broken another valve. The only saving grace that was available to clutch to was that surprisingly, I had taken the forethought in Houston to buy spare valve to carry with me for just such an occasion. Looking about me for inspiration I knew that now of course, I was landed with the problem that I had had on previous breakdowns, which simply boiled down to a severe lack of tools to get the job done. Upon searching out the darkest corners of my brain for a solution, I struck on the small memory of seeing a classic car centre on the road to the Hostel, which if memory served me correctly was only about a mile away. We chugged our way down to the workshop and as had now become quite usual, they were rather surprised to see an East coast Morris with an English driver. I spoke to the proprietor who turned out to also be an Englishman, and to both our great surprise was also originally from my hometown of Rochford in Essex, where his parents like mine still live. After a deal of reminiscing between us, the conclusion was come to that his insurance wouldn't allow me to do the work on Horris on his premises, but I was kindly more than welcome to use his tools to do the work by the side of the road outside his compound. I set to work on my machine with a passion, hoping to complete the job with a splendid deal of pace, and within a trice the cylinder head was sitting on the floor ready for inspection. Once again it was the same valve that had burnt out. My mind found this to be annoyingly strange and I couldn't quite comprehend why this one always seemed to give the trouble. After expending a few minutes partaking in thinking and contemplation, I chose to give the new valve an extremely good lap in and put all the components back together again. Before the head was replaced I fitted two head gaskets at the same time to lower the compression ratio, which hopefully would help stop the destruction of the valves situation occurring again.

With everything back together again and the tools that I had borrowed from my friends in the classic car workshop gratefully returned, Horris was once more ready to roll. Also In an attempt to think ahead to the next breakdown, I left an order with the chaps in the garage to try and procure another valve for me during the day. The only foreseeable problem that immediately came to mind was that it was now the18th of December, and most normal people would be starting to wind down for Christmas, and no doubt their interest in Morris valves at this time would be moderately low.

The afternoon arrived on time again as expected, so as Horris was now up and running to his near full health levels, we motored off with a sprightly pace to inspect with relish the Queen Mary and the Spruce Goose aeroplane which were parked next to one another in Long Beach. The next thirty minutes found me engaged in the drive to my destination, where I gave myself a huge surprise when actually managing to find them without the aid of a map, without getting seriously lost, and without too much trouble! Amazing!

The Spruce Goose built by Howard Hughes and the largest aeroplane ever to fly, now lives inside a huge dome much like a caged animal in a zoo. Upon reflection I suppose this sounds a little silly to say, but to see something so enormous that was designed to fly trapped within its own protective cupola, in a kind of mechanical stasis was quite sad to behold. The aeroplane itself though was tremendously impressive; I completed the obligatory climb over, under and inside of the fuselage, and even several laps around the outside while simply trying to get the measure of its enormous size. When I had finished my jaw dropping exploration of the Goose, my legs carried me onwards towards the Queen Mary to have an examination of her majestic interior. While on the stroll back from seeing the aircraft a walkway was crossed leading onto the ship. Here much to my utter shock, my eyes glanced downward to Horris only to discover

that he had disappeared from the parking bay on the side of the road
where he had been left only a couple of hours before. Rushing back, my
mind pondered the terrible thoughts that some international Morris
thieves had stolen him away. As I ran my brain toyed with the thoughts
that he was probably being hauled onto a ship ready to be put in the secret classic car collection of an Arabian Sheikh! While making haste towards his previous location I found myself clearing flights of stairs in one
go, leaping fences, and vaulting walls, such was my alarm! It was only
when I came skidding up to where I had left him, or should I say
"thought" I had left him that I noticed a huge Jeep had been quite inconsiderately parked behind Horris. This American leviathan completely
dwarfed my friend and hid him within its enormous shadow, so much so
that I'm sure a whole new ecosystem started to evolve on various parts of
my car! Moving the Morris directly behind the jeep I hoped to at least get
a little revenge confusion on its ridiculous owners and also keep Horris
within my by now much relieved sight.

The Queen Mary is unquestionably a seriously impressive liner. Having
only ever been on cross channel ferries before, I was quite taken aback by
the huge size and the general magnificence of the vessel as she lay there
by the harbour side. Choosing to climb down numerous steps to the engine room area had me blustering for breath, but knowing this was the
region that fascinated me the most made it an unquestionably worthwhile
trip.

The rooms were full of bells, whistles, lovely big brass handles and instruments, great levers protruded from panels which no doubt opened
and closed some very important ship type things deep within the boat's
internal workings. Reminiscing about all the old ocean liner related films
from my youth, the gaze from the eyes landed upon the round handles
protruding from the ceiling. Were these, my imagination queried, the very
handles that desperate sailors would spin round in an attempt to stop
blown out valves and ruptured tanks from sinking their ship. Evidently
the Queen Mary hadn't been at panic stations for quite some time because all of her levers and knobs were quite unyielding to the touch and
turn of a motoring Morrisman. Again I reflected on the beauty of taking
the journey in December. On almost all occasions, whichever exhibit or
monument I was to attend, I found myself with no bothersome crowds
and the engine room on this vast ocean going vessel was to be no excep-
tion to this rule. A good hour was spent sailing the seven seas and having
many a brave adventure against all the odds that nature and pirates could
throw at me. When it was time to leave, to be quite honest I couldn't

really remember the correct positions of everything I had been playing with. So the next ten minutes found me engaged in winding everything up and pulling on all the levers, in the assumption that like a car's handbrake, things that are pulled on will stop it rolling, or in the case at hand, floating or sinking away! When setting foot on dry land once more, I came to the conclusion that becoming a sailor was not to be ever taken up as a serious career option for myself. As much as I enjoyed my time in the engine room it was far too cramped for my liking, and the thought of being stranded in there with a whole load of sweaty fellow shipmates, to be quite honest, rather put me off the whole idea. My path led me back down to Horris where I noticed that the jeep had graciously moved away. Lucky for them that we didn't get to encounter one another, as I would have had to engage in a caustic comment regarding their irresponsible parking practices.

Trundling back towards the Hostel I called in to the Classic car centre to see if they had any luck procuring me some valves. With regret fate wasn't smiling on me regarding the valves, as they couldn't receive any before Christmas. Taking the news on the chin I thanked them and settled on trying to perhaps acquire another valve on the way to San Francisco. Booking in for another night at the hostel my plans were laid out for the following day, a trip to Disneyland and Hollywood was definitely on the cards and afterwards turn to the north and head towards San Francisco. As the sun set over the Pacific Ocean my inspection of the speedo revealed that we had covered a stunning 25 miles.

CHAPTER

TWENTY SEVEN

Big Kids

I was up with the larks in the morning and all excited as it was the day of a visit the place that all big kids dream of, Disneyland! Meeting three Aussies in the hostel the previous night proved fortuitous as I managed to scrounge a lift with them in their tremendous old yank tank. It also gave Horris a days rest as well, for which I'm sure he was equally thankful. Pulling into Disneyland is initially anyway, like pulling into a huge great carpark. You have to firstly cross a great expanse before getting to the actual front door of the grounds. The thought of having to leave my car and then walk all the way across this vast region when visiting in the summer, then having to try and find your way back again would I'm sure overtax my mental functions.

When entering through the gates I'm sure I didn't know what to expect from this world famous palace of fun, but my childish dreams were not to be disappointed. There was an immense range of differing rides and shows, no real roller coasters per se, but definitely enough for a notable experience. All the areas within the outer walls are based on different lands, Futureland, Marineland, etc, with vast displays in each, consisting of remarkable Jim Henson style puppets singing and dancing as you move on through. We made our way to one show that was based in a small old time style theatre. As we were seated waiting for the curtain to come up, my senses didn't really take much notice of the Moose and Reindeer heads hanging upon the wall. After a few short moments people started noticing that their eyes were moving about and looking at the audience. All of a sudden, in the way of a magician waving his wand they came to life, started to heckle the people in the theatre and also throw many an insult at each other! It was a truly marvellous double act and I had to almost pinch myself afterwards to remember that they weren't actually real. They did steal the show though, as memory fails me regarding anything of the performance that was on the stage. After seeing the animal double act we jumped on the monorail to head to the other side of the park. The ride was incredibly brisk, yet smooth and rather more pleasant and genial than using a train. The last particularly notable ride upon which we took an excursion was a submarine, which carried us on an underwater journey around the world. Diving down below the ocean, while peering out of the tiny porthole at the corals and plants I felt bestowed with the eyes of submariners and adventures of yesteryear in their quest for undersea knowledge. Topside again, the group unanimously agreed to a man, that the journey had been thoughtfully realistic and extremely impressive.

We spent from 9 o'clock in the morning to about 7 o'clock in the evening within the grounds at Disney, and even then we didn't get to see everything. It had cost us $25 each to gain admittance and was certainly well worth the expense. Stopping off for a frightful burger supper, we sat round a table and eulogised like a group of schoolchildren on the days exciting events. The exuberance only ceased when we arrived back at the hostel and a more macho demeanour came over us! At the end of the fine days excursions a restful Horris at least, had covered no fatiguing miles!

CHAPTER

TWENTY EIGHT

It Must Be a Sign!

It was to be an important photo session day today, as we were heading up to the famous Hollywood sign for some pictures. Leaving the hostel it only took about thirty minutes for me to spot the sign sitting up there on the hillside, I had found to my utter amazement that my navigation skills had appeared to greatly improve since entering the Los Angles area. Why this should be I'm not absolutely sure, maybe it was down to the local way of laying out the roads and signposts. Whatever it was though, I was enjoying, what to me was quite a novel experience. Wending my way to the base of the hill I stopped and entered into what seemed like a restaurant. The room was full of rather well to do women covered in gold jewellery and substantially serious hairdo's, while wearing the stretched appearance of plastic surgery. They seemed to be having a bit of a local "woman's institute" meeting or the American equivalent which soon stopped when my dishevelled form entered the room. An expeditious smile and "hello" soon found them at their ease when they realised that I had no intention of murdering them. With my inquiries made I was sent on my way with coffee, some cake and the obligatory directions.

Apparently you are unable to drive to within handling distance of the sign any more. Thus educated, I then had to find a location with a good line of sight for taking the photograph from the roadside. We set off up the maze of tiny narrow winding roads which spread up and around the hills, many times we had to turn about and retrace our steps as we headed off in the wrong direction, but in the end we happily managed to encounter a most admirable position for our picture.

Hollywood!

The photograph taken, Horris and I made our descent from the hills and immediately made an acquaintance with the Route101 heading north for San Francisco. The road followed the coast up past Santa Barbara then on to San Luis Obispo where it turned inland to follow a more direct route to my objective. Trundling along the freeway in the quest of a Motel for the evening, I was soon surrounded by a plethora of suitable establishments only a few miles south of Salinas. Signing into the cheapest room for my noontide slumbers I felt relief as by now my person was quite haggard and worn. The previous evening my fellow hostel dwellers and I had been kept awake by an incredible snorer for most of the night, and now it had finally caught up with me. Another predicament was now beginning to rear its ugly head, Horris' transmission was starting to vibrate rather badly and make horrible grinding noises in the gearbox area. I only hoped it would last long enough to get us to San Francisco. At the days end while sitting and soaking in a lovely hot bath I noted that we had covered another 142 miles.

CHAPTER

TWENTY NINE

Vibrations from below

My lovely beauty sleep in a nice large bed was something that I most certainly appreciated during the night, and with nobody snoring for a gold medal as well, it proved to be a delight! The outlay was difficult to accept in the wallet region at $25, but the bed, shower and bath made me feel so much better I felt it was well worth the extra cost. A stroll was taken from the motel to the local restaurant to engage in a light breakfast, which I thought would help the finances a little. Here unfortunately my rumbling stomach got the better of me again, and I ended up gorging like a starved wolf, forcing me to spend a huge $8 on my breakfast! In my stomach's defence, I must say that there was a great deal of food dished out for the $8 and I scoffed it all down and felt even better for it afterwards.

I now had a new rush of energy flowing inside me which was good as Horris unfortunately didn't, for the vibration now had become really quite appalling. After giving it a great deal of thought I concluded that there was no way that we were going to be able to make it any further than San Francisco without a new gearbox and propshaft. By the time that we had arrived in the downtown area our speed was restricted to a paltry 30 miles per hour with huge metallic clunks and grinding noises coming from below poor old Horris' floor. At this moment the realisation came over me that we were at journey's end. Finding the replacement parts would be hard enough at a normal time of the year, but it was now only two days before Christmas and my money was also rapidly running out. A small amount of disappointment came upon me as I had intended to try and make it all the way back across the Rockies to Toronto in time for the festivities. But the thought of ending up stuck on top of a Rocky with an inoperable gearbox in the freezing snow really didn't seem all that appealing or altogether that safe. We had arrived at our final destination. On reflection I soon accepted that any disappointment that lay within my mind should be immediately shown the way to the door, as we had had a tremendous journey and Horris had done us both extremely proud.

The next task was to try and find some kindly travel agent who would be willing to sell me an extremely cheap air ticket back to London, so downtown Horris and I chugged, to find my passage home. I left Horris parked up in a side street that I had carefully selected to prevent him from being towed away. This was accomplished by walking up and down checking all the signs for a hundred yards either side of the parking position. Also my apprehension led me to ask everybody and anybody who was nearby their opinion on the likelihood of me finding my car removed upon my return, until I was finally satisfied that the car would be safe.

On foot now I set out on a trail of the travel agents. The horrendous prices they were asking for one way tickets was starting to get my person almost a little worried as I beat a weary path to their doors. A feeling of perhaps also a little guilt started to come over me regarding the cost of the large and expensive lunch which I had consumed earlier in the day and how this might now come back to haunt me. Leaving one particularly expensive agents doorway, I entered the street outside with my hand on my forehead looking skyward for inspiration. Amazingly, it miraculously appeared in the shape of a young lady who commented on how ridiculously high the prices were in the shop that I was just leaving. My immediate reply was of course how much I agreed with her statement and did she know of any splendid bucket shops which all cities possess somewhere. She was more than happy to help and led me off up the road to a secret address that she knew. After traversing what seemed like an exceptional number of streets we arrived at a tall, scruffy and dirty building with flaking paint all about. Scaling innumerable flights of stairs as the lift wasn't working she deposited me at the door of San Francisco's "best" cheap flight centre, then disappeared off back down the stairs, and with a wave of the hand she was gone. I knocked on the door and half an hour later found myself the relieved owner of a ticket back to London and $258 lighter in the pocket. One good thing was that the flight landed at 12:30pm on Christmas Eve local time, and as my family didn't actually know I was going to be coming back for the festivities my hope was that it would give them quite a Christmas surprise!

The next sad activity was to search through the yellow pages for a suitable place to sell my faithful friend. Here I discovered a classic car centre in the downtown area that seemed suitable for the purpose. Taking down the address I resolved to head over there in the morning and do the terrible deed. Having learnt such an awful lot over the past year on this continent and during this fabulous journey it seemed most strange that it was all nearly at an end. The only regret, which weighed heavily on my shoulders, was the fact that I had to sell Horris, but unfortunately I really had very little choice in the matter. Chugging back to the hostel we had clocked up a further 26 Morrising miles.

CHAPTER

THIRTY

Sell Your Friend, Go To Jail

Rising even before the larks, I was out of the hostel door by nine o'clock in the morning. As I walked over to where Horris had been parked, the realisation came over me that this was going to be the final drive that we would be taking together. The lump in my throat was exceptionally real. This car had accompanied me through a whole gamut of experiences, starting with my elation when I first purchased him, onto the struggle of getting him roadworthy while parked in the open of a Canadian winter. The sunshine arrived and we hit the highways and byways of Toronto. We had much joyous driving and all the time he never let me down. Into the journey through America he carried me, meeting the people and seeing the places that I had only ever read about or seen on the television. On the way we did have a few mechanical problems and it was one of these and a lack of funds that now caused the end of the journey. My gratitude to old Horris the Morris Minor for sharing this adventure with me can never be measured; the feelings were now part of my being.

I started Horris for the last time and as always he came to life on the first turn of the key. Graunching noises from down below accompanied us downtown to the Classic car centre where I pulled up and parked in front of their workshop. Looking through the open doors I immediately spotted a shiny circa 1950's two seater Maserati sitting there in all its glory. This was surrounded by a variety of other exotic European machinery so happiness overcame me knowing that Horris would be in such good company.

A hasty conversation with the owner immediately gave me the impression that he didn't want to be spending any money on another car only a few days before Christmas. This of course didn't help my bargaining position; the other problem was that Horris probably had only another couple of miles left in him at that moment. If we were to break down on the road the funds were so low he would probably have to be abandoned to his fate at the roadside, which would no doubt mean ending his days in the local scrapyard. With this in mind I gave in and sold him for a monstrously low sum to the owner of the Classic car centre. Slowly I removed his plates and the boss from the centre of the steering wheel to keep as souvenirs, and was then kindly driven down to the harbour with a heavy heart by his new owner to catch the ferry over the water to Alcatraze.

On the way down to the ferry port we passed many of the rather badly damaged buildings that were left over from the recent earthquake. All the overhead concrete highways were closed due to large cracks appearing within their structures. Most of the buildings here also seemed to be filled with these self same cracks, which is not all that surprising really considering what they recently went through. My memories went back to the terrible scenes shown on the TV at the time of the quake, cars and people totally crushed down to a few inches high when the roads collapsed upon them. On this calm winters day the thought of this horror happening here seemed a million miles away.

Soon after being dropped off I caught the boat out across the cold and uninviting San Francisco Bay to a cheerless looking Alcatraz for the sum of $7.00. At the moment of standing on the ferry my mind was made up that there was no way anyone could possibly escape across the icy waters and swim to the shoreline, so sorry Clint, but the film was great!

Putting myself in the place of a prisoner for a few moments, I wondered how you would be feeling heading for the desolate rock before you. Accepting the realisation that you would never probably be coming back again must have been remarkably hard to embrace. When the convicts arrived at their new home I guess, or hope at least, that a touch of regret crossed their minds as they stepped off the boat for the last time. Somewhere along the line these people had made an extremely bad choice in their lives and had ended up committing some terrible crimes. Murderers or rapists were, I think the main occupants of the island, so very little sympathy can be given for the harsh lives that they must have led imprisoned in Alcatraze. Inside the walls of the penitentiary the desolate gloom was even worse than on the outside. The all-pervading damp from the sea air instilled the place with the feeling of desperation and death. This sense clung to the walls and the bars of the building as you moved on through. Passing the cells, which had been used in the film, you can see where they had chipped away the ventilation grills to try and escape. It made you wonder why every person in the place hadn't tried this or another method to gain their freedom.

The solitary confinement cells were in a perverse way possibly almost a relief for the people inside them. The guilty were kept in total darkness where at least they avoided the sights of everyday horror that befell their fellow inmates. Conceivably the solitude let them drift further into the escape of human madness, as this and death would be the only real escape from Alcatraz. Whilst on the return from the island, I stood at the front of the boat with the chill wind blowing upon my face and enjoyed the sensation of pulling into the harbour and jumping down once again onto solid ground. I'm sure it was a feeling that all of the inmates constantly dreamed off back at Alcatraz in their tiny cells. Perhaps though that was the price they deservedly paid for their crimes.

At this moment I in a strange way felt moderately lost. Normally at this juncture in the proceedings I would have the safety of my faithful friend in which to fit like a key in a lock, but now I found myself on my own and it did feel rather peculiar indeed. Strolling down through Fisherman's Wharf I stopped off and had some lunch in a small restaurant. The seafood helped to heal the pangs that were coming from my stomach, but didn't help the ones my heart was feeling for my missing Morris. Heading back along the wharf my person then called in at the Naval Museum that is situated not far from the hostel, and although quite small by Greenwich standards, it did prove to be rather interesting. Walking around now feeling perhaps a little bewildered, I found my way into a local park where sitting down with a recently acquired cup of piping hot coffee the mind had a bit of a reflection about the past month on the road. We had met lots of different travelling people on the journey, all of them taking their own unique routes and methods for getting to their destinations; for myself though, having the freedom that comes with the use of your own motorcar had made the world of difference on a day to day basis. The thought of having to abide to bus or train routes and timetables would be most unappealing, and loosing the independence of being able to turn left or right purely on a whim I now know would surely never do. The other point is that Horris had acted as "home" no matter where we had ended up stopping for the night and I was eternally grateful to him for providing this service on many an occasion.

CHAPTER

THIRTY ONE

Planes, Trains, and Fall Down a Hill

Last day in North America.

The day dawned bright and cold and standing there in the dormitory of the hostel I had a small problem of packing my accumulated goods and chattels that had been unloaded from Horris the day before. After a few rather unsuccessful attempts I managed with the use of a good deal of string to attach just about everything to my rucksack that couldn't be carried in my hands. The hands were already full with a large bag in one, and a box containing a trumpet in the other. The trumpet had been bought in a junk shop in Toronto almost a year before with the good intention of learning how to play. The plan had, as it turned out, never really got beyond the buying of the trumpet stage, so perhaps I could while away a few of the coming hours and start to have a practise on the return flight!

The shuttle bus duly turned up at its designated time and collected its motley crew of returning vagabonds to various parts of the world. We were delivered to the airport at eleven o'clock, which pleased me, as my flight wasn't until five p.m. It was a good job that I like airports!

Come departure time I had chosen a nice window seat that wasn't overlooking the wing. This had been easy to book, as I had probably been the first person to check in for the flight. As we rolled out onto the runway many thoughts of the past year and especially the last month flooded through my mind. All the sights I had seen, experiences gained and the people that I had met were all there in the forefront of my mind. Without doubt I was returning to England as a different person.

With a huge roar of the engines and a fear inspiring vibration shuddering through the aeroplane we accelerated down the runway, then we were up, we were away and then we were finally gone. At this moment, all I could feel was sadness as my adventure was nearly over. After a few hours though of flying along at 30,000 feet I turned my mind to the fact that I was returning home. The prospect of seeing all my family and friends once again was very exciting and especially as the last thing they were expecting me to do was arrive home on Christmas Eve.

Landing in London Heathrow ten hours after leaving San Francisco, the first thing I noticed was the different cars and the number plates that they wore driving about the airport. This is something I have always seen as the first recognition of a new country when travelling by aeroplane. Looking out of the window when you pull round to the terminal, the new people and vehicles always stand out. The strange thing on this occasion though was that they still looked strange even though it was my home. By the time I had collected up my rucksack and bags and found my way down to the tube station my body was completely exhausted. Soon, realisation came upon me that there was no way I could remove the rucksack from my back as due to the weight and the lack of energy in my body I wouldn't be able to get it back on again. In the airport I had to enlist the help of a couple of friendly Yankees to get it on in the first place, so on it would have to stay until I arrived home. Thankfully it being the day before Christmas the trains weren't too busy so by sitting sideways I could almost feel reasonably comfortable. A disaster nearly occurred while going up one of the escalators when my balance went and I nearly found myself toppling over backwards to my doom. Only frantic grabbing of the rails on my part managed to save my extremely tired neck from ending up broken on the floor. Leaving Liverpool Street station it was now only a further hour and a half ride on the direct train line before I was home. It seemed to last forever but as the familiar station names started to appear it helped to boost my flagging reserves. When we finally pulled onto the Rochford platform I was mightily relieved. Walking through the station the view of my hometown appeared before me. Now a choice had to be made. Did I give my parents a call and get them to come and pick me up, or should I walk the two miles to their house instead. After a bit of soul searching my feet carried me away from the phone box to walk the path home, purely because it seemed the right thing to do. Although I was walking, there were no rules making me adverse to taking any possible shortcut that may come my way. The first of these arrived at the bottom of the station road, instead of walking around on the tarmac path it was possible to cut the corner off by walking down the grassy bank. It was dark, it was wet, and the bank was muddy, one step out and away I went end over end rolling down through the mud thinking on the way what a good idea it had been! Standing up was now the only problem I seemed to have. Luckily for me there was a set of railings alongside the pavement on which my rolling body had come to rest. Using these I thankfully managed to haul myself back up onto my feet and stagger off on my way. Walking along, the weight of the pack on my back and the bags in my hands were definitely starting to take a toll. Every couple of hundred yards I had to stop to catch a breath and have a bit of a rest. All I felt like doing at this moment was sleeping. I came to the next shortcut on my itinerary, Tinkers Lane. This was an unmade road with thick bushes on either side, and no lights or houses anywhere along its length. Halfway down I managed to find the footpath stile hidden amongst the trees. Here I had a good five-minute rest to try and regain some energy. Sitting there looking at the stars I found it amazing that on that very same morning I had been in San Francisco and now here I was on an old muddy road in Rochford upon which I had cycled and walked many times since I was a child. Setting off again I passed the Car breakers yard where in the past many a happy hour had been spent rummaging through looking for spare parts. Gazing through the fence I could ironically see two different Morris Minors waiting to be stripped for spares. If I could have had these at my disposal over the past year my life would have been a great deal easier, and also a great deal less expensive to boot. My mind was made up that my last stop would be a sit down on the steel box section fence a hundred yards from the entrance of the industrial estate that I was now leaving. Here another good ten minutes rest was taken and then my feet carried me off on the final leg of my walk.

My arms, shoulders and legs were numb as rounding the final bend, home came into sight, the lights were on which made me rather thankful that my parents hadn't gone out for the evening. I drew level with the house and went to cross the road and in the process nearly got run over due to looking the wrong way. That would have been a great finish to my travels'. Pulling the bell pull for I had forgotten to take my keys when I left, I waited. The dog barked, the door opened, I was home.

My further adventures can be found at
www.pennyfarthingworldtour.com

Printed in the United Kingdom
by Lightning Source UK Ltd.
103001UKS00001B/118